WITHDRAWN

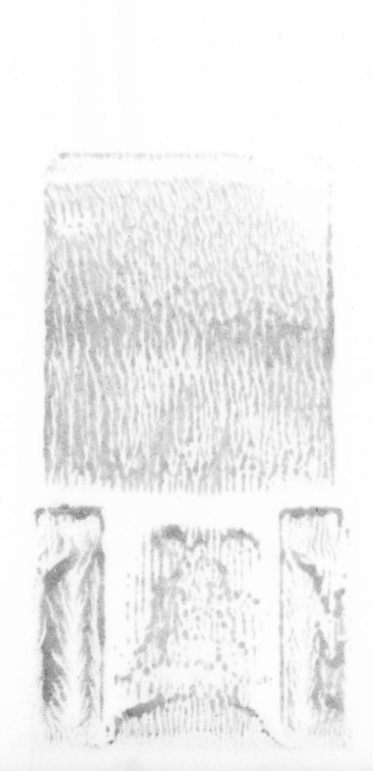

My
Appalachia

My Appalachia

A
reminiscence
by
Rebecca
Caudill

Photographs
by
Edward
Wallowitch

Holt, Rinehart and Winston
New York Chicago San Francisco

Acknowledgments

Many persons helped me in the writing of *My Appalachia*. To all of them I am deeply grateful.

Burton and Mary Rogers of Pine Mountain Settlement School, Pine Mountain, Kentucky, offered me their generous hospitality, shared my interest in this book, and gave me many helpful suggestions for its development.

Dr. Wilson Evans, Dean of Labor, Berea College, Berea, Kentucky, arranged valuable interviews for me. Dr. Lawrence S. Thompson of the University of Kentucky, Lexington, provided me with printed material pertaining to the Southern Appalachians.

The following persons generously provided me with information about their particular areas of the Southern Appalachians and gave me insights into the lives of the people in the areas: Miss Lula M. Hale, Homeplace, Ary, Kentucky; Mr. Perley F. Ayer, Executive Director, and Mr. Loyal Jones, Associate Executive Director, of the Council of the Southern Mountains, Berea, Kentucky; Miss Ella Crawford, Miss Ceveline Jackson, Miss Jean Lamb, Miss Carolyn Keith, Mr. Ronald Mattson, and Mr. Dean Meadows, all students of Berea College; Dr. W. D. Weatherford, Black Mountain, North Carolina; Dr. and Mrs. Lundy Adams, Blackey, Kentucky; Mrs. Jalia Turner Sebastian and Mr. and Mrs. Roscoe Sebastian, Booneville, Kentucky; Mr. and Mrs. Robert Connor and Mr. Brittle Courtney, Bluefield, West Virginia; Miss Mary Wright, Buckhorn, Kentucky; Mr. and Mrs. Dean Cadle, Mr. and Mrs. Larry Craft, and the Reverend Ed French, Cumberland, Kentucky; Miss Pat Edwards, Dayton, Ohio, formerly of Speedwell, Tennessee; Mr. and Mrs. Shirley Langford, Field, Kentucky; Mr. and Mrs. Dan Gibson and Mr. Paul Ashley, Cockle Trace of Clear Creek, Fisty, Kentucky; Mr. Tom Gaston, Fort Knox, Kentucky; the late Mr. Granville Cornett, Hurricane Gap, Kentucky; Mrs. Billie Jean Cawood, Harlan, Kentucky; Dr. Margaret Livengood and Mrs. Francie Hager, Hazard, Kentucky; Mr. Raymond McLain, Hindman, Kentucky; Mr. James Still, Morehead, Kentucky; Mr. and Mrs. Alvin Boggs, Mrs. Delia Creech, Miss Mildred Mahoney, Mr. and Mrs. Levi Merrill and family, Mr. and Mrs. Jesse Patterson, Mr. Brit Wilder, and Mr. and Mrs. Jerry Workman, Pine Mountain, Kentucky; State Senator Durham W. Howard, Pineville, Kentucky; Mrs. Rosa Belle Kirk Evans, St. Charles, Virginia; Mrs. Poppy Ann Adams, Mr. and Mrs. Harry Caudill, and Mr. Tom Gish, Whitesburg, Kentucky.

Sister Mary Evelyn Eaton of the Glenmary Sisters of Chicago and Miss Pat Edwards shared with me their experiences in working with Southern Appalachian families that have migrated to large cities. Mrs. Wendell C. Goddard of Grosse Point Farms, Michigan, Miss Marian Kingman of Berea, Miss Margaret B. Motter of Frederick, Maryland, and Mrs. John K. Orndorff of Sewickley, Pennsylvania, all formerly teachers at the Pine Mountain Settlement School, assessed for me the quality of life in the Kentucky mountains before coal became the dominant industry. Mrs. Stella Caudill Sutton, my eldest sister, of Tifton, Georgia, supplied me with information about my birth and the family history of my earliest years.

United States Senators Paul Douglas of Illinois and John Sherman Cooper of Kentucky provided me with copies of the Appalachian Regional Development Act and other federal government publications necessary to the writing of this book. Assistant Attorney General David A. Schneider of the Commonwealth of Kentucky gave me information concerning the status of long-form deeds in Kentucky courts.

I wish to express special thanks to photographer Edward Wallowitch for his keen interest in this book and for his good companionship as a traveler through the rugged Southern Appalachians; to my husband, James Ayars, professional editor, always my severest and best critic, who encouraged and helped me in every phase of the planning and writing of *My Appalachia;* and to Mr. Arthur A. Cohen and his staff at Holt, Rinehart and Winston. Mr. Cohen's encouragement, constructive criticism, and patience have been mine throughout the writing of this book.

Urbana, Illinois
May 18, 1966

Rebecca Caudill

Published simultaneously in Canada by Holt, Rinehart and Winston of Canada, Ltd.

Library of Congress Catalog Card Number: 66-21620

Grateful acknowledgment is made to the following for permission to reprint excerpts from their publications:

Council of the Southern Mountains, Inc., for a portion of "The Weaknesses Are Appearing" by Larry Greathouse from the Fall, 1965, issue of *Mountain Life & Work*

The Viking Press, Inc. for "Heritage" from HOUNDS ON THE MOUNTAIN by James Still, copyright, 1937, 1965 by James Still

Design:
Stanley Davis and Anthony Aviles
Davis-Aviles Graphic Design, Inc.

81321-2116
Printed in the United States of America

In memory of Arah

1

The Day Before Yesterday

My twin sister and I, so I have been told, were assisted on our arduous journey into life by a midwife, Usley Boggs. This event took place at Poor Fork, Kentucky, on a bitter cold night in early February. Three days later my sister died.

My father hammered together a coffin of pine boards in which to bury my sister and covered it with black cambric.

One of our neighbors, Cassie Huff, came across our pasture, bringing with her a tiny dress and a dainty pillow of soft white mull, together with a length of the same material. With the length of mull she made for my sister's coffin a lining, gathering the material into a softness at the bottom and around the sides. Then she laid the pillow in the coffin for my sister's head to rest on and prepared my sister for burial.

My father laid my sister in the black-sheathed coffin, gently, as if he feared he might disturb her last, long sleep. Then he nailed the cover on the coffin, lifted the burden to his shoulder, and, bearing a much heavier burden within himself, set out across the Poor Fork River on the ice for the Sand Hill graveyard on the opposite side.

Neighbor men had already dug a grave —such a little grave!—in which to lay the coffin. Respectfully and silently they stood and watched my father lay his child in the grave. Then my father stood with head bowed while the neighbors shoveled earth on the coffin, gently and quietly. When they had rounded the earth into a mound, my father brought a small field stone and placed it upright at the head of the grave. A smaller stone he placed at the foot of the grave. No hymn was sung. No prayer was uttered. No word was spoken. Silence proclaimed the grief of my father and the warmth of the neighborly understanding that sustained him.

Their duties finished, my father and his neighbors returned, each to his own home, leaving beneath the little mound not only the cold lifeless body of my sister but a part of my father as well.

Once before my father had performed this sad rite. Twelve years earlier, when he and my mother lived at the head of Sand Lick, a son James, their firstborn, at the age of one and a half years had sickened and wasted away.

In the crumbling old graveyards on the steep Appalachian mountainsides, the preponderance of little mounds repeats the same story—no doctor, no hospital, no visiting nurse, no health services of any kind, not even a drugstore or a druggist. Only the few home remedies —quinine, castor oil, turpentine, and liniment—were to be found on the kitchen shelf, while in every neighborhood the old midwife went her rounds with her baskets and pockets full of herbs gathered on the mountains and her head full of notions about the birthing of babies.

The Appalachia that was mine as a child was a narrow valley in Harlan County. Through the valley ran the Poor Fork of the Cumberland River. High mountains walled the valley, Pine Mountain to the north of us, Big Black to the south. The house in which I lived formed the hub of my world, and the other parts that I knew intimately radiated from the hub like spokes in a wheel.

The earliest memory of my childhood was of an occurrence that took place on the first Tuesday of November when I was two years old. Through this occurrence I was introduced to a facet of life that is embedded in mountain culture like the imprint of a prehistoric fern in a lump of coal.

It was election day. In the mountains of eastern Kentucky, election day when I was a child was a special day on which drinking, quarreling, shooting, feuding, and generally disturbing the peace were anticipated, by some with dread, by others with pleasure, and accepted by all as normal. Eastern Kentucky, as well as the Appalachian sections of other southern states, was overwhelmingly Republican, with only a slight sprinkling of Democrats.

For days preceding the election, men talked of little else. If a Republican candidate for state office thought it worth his time to campaign in the mountain counties, his visit was the occasion for a big spread of home-cooked victuals provided by Republican wives for menfolks only and liquor provided by the candidate— also for menfolks only. The candidate did not need to talk of issues. He needed only to call his Democratic opponent names, and the more stigmatic the names, the louder the applause by his hearers. If, in addition, the candidate could play a fiddle or tell tall tales, he was considered even better qualified for the office he sought, though he would have received all the Republican votes anyway.

The Poor Fork precinct in which we lived was totally Republican except for two dissenters, my father and John Yeary, who, come hell or high water (both of which plagued us often in our community), voted Democratic. Their insistence on voting at every election raised the tempers of Republicans, many of whom, in accordance with mountain custom of the time, appeared at the polls with Colt in holster, cartridges in belt, and bottle in hip pocket.

The polling place was traditionally in Will Cornett's store across the river from our house. The polls opened at six in the morning and closed at six in the evening. Every voter in the precinct was in line when the door was opened, and he stayed at the polling place until the votes were counted. Now and then during the day a few tipsy friends went outside to take an extra dram, stage a shooting match, or race their horses up and down the rocky country roads. Schools were always closed on election days, since no mother considered it safe to allow a child on the road, and womenfolks stayed behind closed doors.

The election that took place when I was two years old was an unusually heated one, a special election called to choose a governor to succeed William Goebel. Goebel was an ambitious Democratic politician who, in the election of the previous year, had been declared governor even though he had received a minority of the votes. Just as the Election Commission was about to declare the Republican candidate elected governor, Goebel was shot, presumably by one of four hundred armed mountaineers "visiting" Frankfort at the invitation of Republicans. The Kentucky Assembly, overwhelmingly Democratic, made a hurried recount of the votes and instructed the Election Commission to announce the election of Goebel. The oath of office was administered to Goebel on his deathbed.

Long before election day arrived, my father was notified that he would be shot if he dared show up at the polls. Friends among his Republican acquaintances urged him for once to refrain from voting and to stay at home. But he had a duty to perform, my father informed them—he and John Yearey. One had to serve as judge, the other as clerk, to see that their votes were counted.

Then, cautioned his friends, he ought to buy himself a gun.

"Why?" asked my father, who was the only mountaineer I knew in those days who owned neither bottle nor gun. One man killed at the polls would be quite enough, he said. It didn't improve matters to kill two. He bought no gun.

When election day arrived, my father and mother rose earlier than usual. My father was eating his breakfast by lamplight when the kitchen door, never locked, was suddenly opened, and four Republican friends walked in. Each was fully armed. They told my mother that they had come to take my father to the polls, that they would stand over him all day and bring him safely home at night.

I had wakened early, crawled out of bed, and toddled into the living room, where I saw my mother standing at the window. I went and stood beside her, my chin resting on the windowsill. Though daylight had not yet fully dawned, through the morning mist I could see my father and the other men walking down the road toward the fording place in the river, one man in front of my father, one behind him, and one on either side of him, in the form of a cross.

Suddenly my mother, forgetting me, burst into tears, covered her eyes with her apron, rushed into a closet, and shut the door. I had never before seen my mother cry. In that instant my security vanished, my world fell apart like a tower of blocks, and I, a little child lost, screamed in terror.

My screams awoke my sisters and my brother. Out of bed they jumped and came running, thinking perhaps I had fallen into the fire. In spite of all their affectionate entreaties, I could not tell them why I was crying. I did not know.

In a short time, my mother, her eyes dried, her emotions composed, came out of the closet. She smiled at me, and immediately my world took on its old familiar shape.

It was only as I grew older, and bit by bit, for both my father and mother were innately reserved and rarely shared with us children matters best forgotten, that I knew what was happening that morning.

In spite of the scarcity of Democratic votes in the Poor Fork precinct, the governorship was won by the Democratic candidate, J.C.W.

Beckham, who, as lieutenant governor, had succeeded Goebel. During Beckham's term in office he sent to my father a reproduction of an autographed, impressively imposing portrait of himself which my father pasted on our parlor wall. Governor Beckham, I assumed, was next in command to God.

My father's farm occupied bottom land west of the river. On it were the usual appurtenances—corncrib, stable, smokehouse, hen house—and back of the house was a garden. These were basic to our livelihood. But to mention them and nothing more is like tasting wine that has no flavor.

First of all, in our childhood, there was time, and there was freedom. No one was ever rushed, ever hurried. We children as we grew up had our chores to do. We fed the chickens morning and night; we found nubbins in the corncrib for the cow to eat while she was being milked; we washed and dried the dishes (over which many an argument arose as to who should wash and who should dry); we tacked carpet strings by the mile, it seemed to me, and then admired the multicolored balls when they were rolled up and ready to be woven into a new carpet. But, when we had done our chores, we could play. We could play anything we wanted to play, but, since we had few toys, we usually busied ourselves outdoors.

There was, for instance, the newborn calf that licked our fingers when we stuck them through the cracks of the fence; the baby pigs we watched feeding gluttonously from their mother's teats; the horse we rode home from the field when Mother sent us to tell Father dinner was ready. Father didn't need to be told that dinner was ready. He could tell that by the overhead position of the sun. But Mother, knowing our love of riding the horse home from the field, sent us as a reward for chores well done.

There was, babbling through the meadow, the clear branch in which Clara and I waded in the summertime. Often, with our feet dangling in the water, we stretched lazily on our backs in the lush grass on the banks and watched butterflies and clouds scudding along overhead before the wind.

There was the apple orchard, brooded over by Big Black Mountain, that for a period in springtime was a foamy,

fragrant sea of pinkish cloud. Sometimes Clara and I stood for long periods listening to the cello-like humming of bees among the blossoms. Often we were tempted to climb the low branches and hide ourselves away, but the bees warned us to keep our distance. So we stood and sniffed instead.

A road ran between our house and the river, but it was so seldom traveled that a passerby was a phenomenon to be reported to the rest of the family, who hastily gathered at windows or on the porch to stare.

Sometimes a drover of cattle or sheep came by on his way to market, usually some place across the mountains in tidewater Virginia. Once at dusk a drover arrived at our house with a flock of sheep. He asked my father for lodging for the night and for a place to pen up his sheep. Not only were such requests never refused; they were granted gratis.

I watched with fascination and followed at a distance as my father helped the drover herd the sheep into our barn lot. The animals looked so gentle and so soft and wooly that, undetected by my father, I climbed over the fence into the barn lot to pat one. Unfortunately the one I chose on which to shower my affection was a ram that returned my advances by lowering his head and butting me straight into the corncrib. My screaming brought Father to my rescue.

Our favorite playground was Broomsedge Hill, a cleared section of mountainside that provided recreation both summer and winter. One winter day my sisters and my brother were wrapping up to go sledding when my father said to them, "Take Becky with you." My mother brought a handful of garments she had knit. She wound me up like a cocoon in her long woolen fascinator, shoved a pair of Clara's outgrown mittens on my hands, took off my copper-toed shoes and pulled an extra pair of wool stockings high on my legs, and put my shoes on again. Then we set out.

We had only one sled, made by my father by nailing hickory runners on a big wooden box. The sled was heavy, and Will and Stella took turns pulling it across the snowy pasture and up the mountainside. Clara trudged close behind them. Far in the rear, Cappie, four years my senior, led me by the hand along the tracks made by those ahead of us.

Arrived at the top of the hill, we scrouged into the box. Stella, claiming the privilege by reason of her seniority, and Will, claiming it by reason of his sex, took turns sitting in the back of the box to hold the rope and guide the sled. Cappie sat in front of Stella or Will, and Clara sat in front of Cappie, while I was tucked into the front end of the box, my knees touching my chin, and was held securely around the waist by Clara. A counting of "One, two, three, GO!" and a unified lurching of all in the box set us in motion. Down the long mountainside we flew, the snow screeching under our runners, the icy wind whipping our faces and tingeing our cheeks as red as the leaves of the sourwood tree in autumn.

In summer we built playhouses on Broomsedge Hill. Since we had around us an ample supply of rocks, we built our houses of them.

One summer, Will—always one to strike a bargain or to swap gainfully whatever was in his pockets—bargained with Clara and me that, if we would carry rocks for him, he would let us play in the house he would build. Unversed in bargains, we at once started roaming over the mountainside to look for rocks we could carry.

Will designed his house with three sides of rock piled three feet high and the fourth side left open. When he had built the walls to the desired height, he decided he might as well build a two-story house and let Clara and me occupy the upper story. For this he needed some boards that he remembered were lying behind the stable. He told Clara and me to go down the mountain to fetch them.

Clara had ridden her favorite stick horse up the mountain that morning— a stick from which she had carefully shaved all the bark—and she decided, since the stable was some distance from the playhouse, we should ride down for the boards. I complained that I had no horse to ride, but she told me, somewhat loftily, that I was too little to ride alone anyway and that I should therefore ride behind her.

I climbed on the rail fence to mount, but, since the horse was spirited and not used to carrying double, Clara had difficulty coaxing him to the fence. He cavorted in circles, time after time coming near the fence, but quickly shying away again.

Eventually, I decided that if ever I was going to get on the horse I would have to jump the next time he came near. Jump I did—and I landed on the horse so hard that I broke him in two in the middle.

Clara was furious. Instead of galloping down the mountain, we'd now have to walk, she complained. I couldn't see a great difference between galloping with a stick between our legs, and walking, but I didn't dare say so, not to Clara. So we walked down the mountain for the boards, Clara sulking, I subdued.

While Will laid a floor of the boards, Clara and I were sent to find more rocks for the upper story. Then we were sent down the mountain for another load of boards for the roof.

When finally the playhouse was finished, Clara and I decided we would like a carpet on our floor. We therefore ranged through the woods on the mountain, bringing back in our skirts clumps of brilliant green mosses with which we carpeted our floor, wall to wall.

Since there was nothing more to do, the three of us went to bed. Will curled up in his spacious quarters downstairs, and Clara and I climbed in upstairs and lay down. No sooner had we begun to settle ourselves than Will complained loudly that we were sifting dirt down in his face. "If you've got to have that moss up there, you'll have to be still," he ordered.

Clara and I lay stiff and still in our cramped quarters, afraid to move so much as a finger. Finally, I had to squirm. Both dirt and moss sifted down on Will, and promptly Clara and I, who had done most of the hard work of building the house, were evicted from it.

In winter, the Poor Fork was the playground for all the children living along the river. We had no skates, but the older and more practiced could go sliding long distances and do fancy twirls and figures in their heavy-soled shoes.

The first time my mother let me go skating, I stood on the bank of the river and looked with envy as Clara breezed by, calling patronizingly, "Did Mother say you could come out here, Honey? You'd better run back to the house before you freeze."

My father, who often went skating with the children of the neighborhood, was skating that day. When he caught sight of me, standing at the edge of the river and about to cry, he went immediately to the house and came back carrying Mother's kitchen chair and a blanket. He spread the blanket on the chair, bundled me up in it, and, taking the two posts of the chair in his hands, skated out on the river, pushing me along in front of him.

"Come on, everybody! Let's play crack-the-whip!" someone shouted.

The skaters clasped hands, with Father at one end of the line. Over the ice we flew. Whenever my father stopped quickly, the skaters at the far end of the line would go sprawling on the ice. I felt very important skimming along safely in the chair—until I remembered Clara. I longed to do everything that Clara did. This craving nagged me all of my growing-up years.

The spokes of my small world reached out to the neighbors and the institutions that shared our river bottom. Our nearest neighbors, Jim and Cassie Huff, lived downriver across our pasture from us. Beside their spacious white house stood their store stocked with goods hauled laboriously across Big Black Mountain from Stonega, Virginia, by a sweating, straining team of four horses hitched to a covered wagon. Jim Huff's going was noted by all who lived along the road, and his return, eagerly watched for, meant a gathering of the neighborhood to help him unload his wares and to see what of this and that he had brought back.

Jim Huff brought back little that a body could get along without. For the women's department, it is true, he brought back a few items with eye appeal for ladies, such as my mother, who kept up with the styles through *McCall's* magazine and had a fancy for dainty laces, colorful ribbons, pretty pearl buttons, and cloth of good quality. But for the men there was the usual supply of essentials: horse collars, iron shoe lasts, axle grease for their wagons, axes, hoes, nails, plowshares, plugs of chewing tobacco, and other things they could not produce on their farms.

We did most of our trading at Huffs' store, bartering with eggs, chickens, potatoes, sweet and Irish, hay, corn, calves, firewood, molasses—anything of which we might have a surplus—in

exchange for such goods as we could not ourselves make at home or produce on the farm.

The store was a long, narrow structure with no windows on either side, but with shelves extending on both sides the length of the building. On a table near the door was a showcase where notions were displayed. Beside it stood a cabinet with small drawers in which were kept spools of thread of many colors. Whenever my mother took me to the store with her, I waited in hungry anticipation for some customer coming to choose a spool of thread, for then the drawers were opened and I could see the dazzling rainbow caught in the cabinet.

The back of the store was the domain of men. A big potbellied stove stood in the center of the floor near the back, and around this stove in winter men were always congregated, talking, talking, and spitting tobacco juice on the fender of the stove. This constituted their main social activity.

Whenever I went to the store with my mother, Cassie or Jim invited me to dip into a big glass jar and help myself to rock candy. It was from the Huffs that I learned that a yard measured thirty-seven inches.

A short distance upriver, on the opposite bank and near the fording place, stood the store of Will and Nora Cornett. The Cornetts and their store, however, were not an intimate part of my world, since I seldom was allowed to cross the river, and never alone.

While the Huffs' store served as our trading center, the Cornetts' store served as the nerve center of the community, for not only was the store the polling place for our precinct on election days, but in one corner of the store was tucked the Poor Fork post office.

This was before the days of Rural Free Delivery. Mail arrived at Cornetts' store once a week, the stage of the river determining the day on which it came. About the middle of the week we children began a lookout for the mail carrier. He rode a bedraggled mud-caked horse along his route, which passed in front of our house. Whoever caught the first glimpse of him, with his saddlebags bulging with mail, rushed the word to my mother. Quickly she sent one of the older children across the river for the mail, either on one of our horses or in the rowboat that was the common property

of the community. I don't recall that letters were plentiful, but there was always the weekly edition of the Louisville *Courier-Journal* to bring home, and, once a month, *McCall's* magazine. On the month the annual subscription to *McCall's* was renewed, there was also a free pattern of my mother's selection to bring home.

We who remained at home waited anxiously for the return of our courier, for he would bring with him not only mail from the outside world but information of happenings in the neighborhood. At the store, representatives of every family in the community met as soon as word spread that the mail had arrived, and they tarried till they had exchanged all the neighborhood news—whose old woman was down sick in bed, what tipsy smart aleck had gotten his comeuppance, who had been bitten by a rattlesnake, who had seen a bear on Big Black, whose cow had been killed by lightning, whose dogs had been in a fight, whose younguns had bloody flux, who had cut his foot with an ax while chopping down a tree. The news was invariably bad.

One other neighborhood institution was a part of my small world. That was a gristmill downriver beyond the curve a short distance below the Huffs'. A few times my father took me there with him, I sitting in front of him on the pommel of the saddle while the sack of corn he was taking to be ground, the shelling of which had been a family project the night before, was distributed evenly across the horse's back, behind the saddle.

The gristmill was to me a fearsome place, with its great undershot waterwheel turned by the clear, fast-running water of the Poor Fork. Inside the mill, all was confusion and noise when the corn was poured into the hopper and the huge furrowed upper stone began turning on the fixed furrowed netherstone, and somewhere, quite a distance away, meal flowed from a wooden spout. When the corn was ground, my father paid the miller his toll, one-seventh of the meal, and, with our share of the meal distributed evenly in the sack across the back of the horse, as the corn had been, we rode off toward home.

The miller seemed unlike any of my other acquaintances. Both his face and his clothes were always a dusty white. I do not now recall his name, but I remember that his face was kind, that

he smiled at me often, and sometimes, as I stood clinging to my father's hand, he chucked me under the chin and called me Honey.

Beyond this small, intimate world, I came gradually to know that, hemmed in between Pine Mountain on one side and Big Black on the other, there was a larger world in which were other places and other people. Along Clover Lick and other small creeks that fed the Poor Fork, up far and lonesome hollows, and across lesser mountain ridges were scattered Davises and Holcombs, Snodgrasses and Coldirons, Stallards and Creeches, and Ratcliffes and Blairs. We did not constitute a town, such as Harlan Town, the county seat, but, scattered though we were, we all claimed Poor Fork as home.

I took for granted the high mountains, the narrow, tight creek bottoms, which often were little more than ravines, and the clear licks and creeks, and supposed that all the world was like that which I knew. It was only when I studied geography that I learned how small and how hemmed in was the corner of Appalachia in which I was born, and how wide and big and how varied in its aspects was the world at large. I was even astonished at the immensity of the Appalachians, since my early acquaintance was limited to Pine and Big Black; the latter, the highest peak in Kentucky, I once assumed to be the highest peak on the earth.

The Appalachians, I learned, lay parallel to the Atlantic seaboard as if they were great ridges washed inland and left stranded by the sea, rather than upheavals created by convulsions of the earth. I learned that they ranged from southwest to northeast, raising their heads proudly from the northern part of Alabama to the St. Lawrence in Quebec.

I learned that the Appalachians, geologically, are the oldest mountain range on the continent of North America, predating the Rocky Mountains by many millions of years. North of the Blue Ridge, in Pennsylvania and Ohio, the blanket of ice of the most recent Ice Age left rich soil deposits in wide valleys where farms now flourish. In West Virginia, which is wholly an Appalachian state, and in Kentucky, Tennessee, and Alabama, all of which escaped the Ice Age, the mountains are covered with a thin layer of soil held together by the

matted roots of laurel and rhododendron, hardwood trees and pines. Here and in the Blue Ridge range in North Carolina the rainfall averages from 60 to 80 inches annually.

The part of Appalachia which for many years has been the cause of economic and social concern to the nation covers approximately 130,000 square miles in eleven states from Alabama to New York, and has a population of about ten million people. I learned from my geography that in this particular part of Appalachia are important cities, and that most of the great rivers east of the Mississippi, some of which flow into the Atlantic, others into the Gulf of Mexico, are fed by many a stream beginning as a trickle near the top of some Appalachian peak. Some of these streams played an important part in the annals of our country. Many of their names are like melodious music: the Roanoke and the Pamlico, the Susquehanna and the Shenandoah, the Potomac and the Delaware, the Congaree, the Wateree, and the Pee Dee flowing into the Atlantic; the French Broad and the Clinch, the Monongahela and the Nolichucky, the Hiwassee, the Tuckasegee, and the Tallapoosa flowing into the Gulf.

Until later years this information was to me an abstraction. The Appalachia that was intimately mine centered in Poor Fork and gradually became enlarged through personal relationships to include the tier of counties wedged against the jutting southwest corner of Virginia—Letcher and Pike, in addition to Harlan, and the tier lying immediately to the north of them, Leslie, Perry, and Knott.

The house in which I was born was a two-story, white-clapboarded building with a front porch running the width of it. I remember only vaguely some parts of the house. Three parts of it, however, are as intimately familiar now as they were when I lived in it. One of these was the stairs, another was the porch, and the third was the fireplace.

The stairs ascended to the upper rooms from the kitchen, and a door shutting off the upper part of the stairs left three steps as a piece of the kitchen furniture. Beside these steps was a window through which I could look out across my father's pasture toward the Huffs'. Near the stairs was the kitchen stove. Often I sat on these stairs, chattering away to my mother as

she worked at the stove. I remember how comforting it was (though I took the comfort for granted) to be near my mother, to ask her my endless whys, to watch her work, and to lick the mixing bowls she emptied.

The early days of spring were always days of excitement when my mother placed fifteen eggs under each hen she caught in the act of setting. When the period of incubation was over, she let Clara and me make the rounds with her to see if a small pip had appeared in any egg, or a wettish chicken had emerged from a shell. Days in spring were as apt to be rainy and cold as sunny and warm. The cold, rainy days my mother dreaded. Some hen was sure not to gather her brood under her for adequate shelter, and always after a shower there were half-drowned baby chickens to carry in from the coops, to wrap in rags, and to lay gently in a box behind the stove, where the air was warm and reviving. Clara and I, one of whose duties was to feed the chickens, hunched over these poor waifs in the box, watching and listening anxiously. The sound of one peep, or the moving ever so little of one rag to assure us life was reviving in a baby chicken, sent us hurrying to tell our mother the good news.

Most of the chickens recovered from their damp chill. Those that could not be revived Mother sent Clara and me to bury. Clara had a natural sympathy for anyone or anything that suffered, and, whenever her tears flowed as she dug a hole in the meadow with a hoe and placed the dead chickens in it, so did mine. When the burial rite was over, we roamed across the meadow looking for flowers with which to decorate the grave.

My most vivid recollection of the stairs is connected with an activity I undertook on a wintry afternoon that deepened quickly into gray twilight as great flakes of snow sifted down silently on pasture and road and mountains.

Stella, the oldest of us, had been sent to Harlan Town to attend school at the Presbyterian Academy. She, I am sure, was born to be a teacher and, when she returned home, even before she had got off her fascinator and coat, she started in without so much as a by-your-leave to teach the rest of us everything she had learned. One thing she had learned of which we had never heard was to say a prayer at night.

Will was not about to say a prayer at night. Nor was he impressed with other newfangled ideas with which Stella seemed to have her head filled and with which she was determined to fill ours. Cappie and Clara were somewhat receptive. But I was Stella's star pupil. She needed to repeat to me only two or three times "Now I lay me down to sleep" till I was off to the kitchen stairs to learn the prayer by heart.

Mother was there, moving quietly about in the kitchen as she prepared supper, ready to help me when I faltered. Outside, the snow, unmarred by mark or stain or football, wrapped the earth in peace. Sometimes a flake, exquisite in its lacy geometric pattern, fell on the windowpane beside me, and momentarily I worshiped and forgot to pray. When the last particle of the flake had melted, I started in again on my "Now I lay me."

Everything seemed bound together, and everything was good—my mother nearby, the warmth from the kitchen stove, the pure snow silently falling, and I with a prayer in my head. This childhood memory I have always kept locked away as insurance to draw on when doubts overwhelm, and when worldly disorders, beyond which one cannot see, darken the earth.

That night I knelt beside my bed, as Stella told me I must, to say my prayer. I felt shy about the rite, particularly since Will was laughing at the gullibility with which I swallowed everything Stella had to offer. I, however, have ever been susceptible to flattery, and Stella stood over me and ground out flattery until she won.

For many years after that I never went to bed without first kneeling and whispering "Now I lay me down to sleep"—for many years until I learned that all of life is both prayer and example, and that posture and timing are wholly irrelevant.

Stella also taught me to say *please* and *thank you,* words no one in our part of Appalachia ever used. Perhaps these gracious words were considered uppity and imitative of outlanders.

The porch was unique, so far as my experience goes. I have never seen another like it, in or out of Appalachia. Someone, maybe my father, or perhaps my mother, decided a bit of decoration would add charm to the porch as a place for sitting on hot summer afternoons or in the long summer twilights. The porch ceiling had been painted white, and, while the paint was still wet, some pioneer in op art had held a lighted kerosene lamp, without a globe, close to the ceiling. The smoke from the unguarded flame made dark gray curlicue patterns with rounded heads and thin, briefly curled tails on the wet paint. The over-all design looked somewhat like a thousand giant commas, pied. I often lay for long periods on my back on the floor, studying the commas, feeling great satisfaction with them.

The fireplace served not only as our heating system, but also, particularly in the winter evenings, as the center of our social activities. Fire-building was a ritual with my father, and the fires he built with huge backsticks that lasted sometimes a week would claim no kinship with the anemic ornamental fires of today.

After supper we all gathered about the fire, my mother, a small woman, sitting in her preferred low chair in one corner, usually piecing a quilt, crocheting lace, knitting stockings, or tacking carpet strings. My father sat in a rocking chair well back from the fire, and the rest of us assorted ourselves wherever we pleased. Two younger sisters, Blanche and Alma, were born in the same house as I, and our favorite place for assorting ourselves was in my father's lap. Always one child was in his lap, usually two, and often three. He accommodated us all with grace.

Sometimes Mother and Father told us stories of their childhoods. Often we pressed Father to tell us about his ancestors. That they had come from England we knew. Had we realized that somewhere in the past there was a mystery, we would no doubt have pressed harder. The name Caudill is of Spanish origin, but my father, tall, fair of complexion, blue-eyed, and sandy-haired, had all the appearance of a true Anglo-Saxon. In reply to every question about ancestry, we always received the same answer: "It doesn't matter nearly so much who you are as what you are." There the questioning ended. I doubt if my father knew who he was.

The argument as to the origin of Appalachian people has been carried on in higher circles than that about our fireplace. Historians John Fiske and Charles and Mary Beard held the opinion that the majority of the people stranded in the mountains were of Scotch-Irish or Ulster Scotch blood. To support their claim are many names of Scotch origin on Revolutionary War muster rolls from mountain areas, and in early records of marriages in these areas.

Between 500,000 and 600,000 Scotch-Irish, driven from Ulster by British oppression, had arrived in the New World by 1776. Many of them may have settled in the mountains, inasmuch as all coastal lands had been taken up.

At least one historian takes the view that parts of the mountains were settled by "shiftless people who could not make a place for themselves in Virginia society, including many of the 'mean whites.'"

Alexander Spotswood, colonial governor of Virginia, wrote in 1717: "The inhabitants of our frontiers are composed generally of such as have been transported hither as Servants, and being out of their time . . . settle themselves where Land is taken up . . . that will produce the necessarys of Life with little Labour. It is pretty well known what Morals such people bring with them hither, which are not like to be much mended by their Scituation, remote from all places of worship."

Whatever the origin of Appalachian mountaineers, it was left for Governor Dunmore, the last of the colonial governors of Virginia, to pin on some of them a description which is as characteristic of Americans today as when, on the Eve of Christmas, 1774, he wrote despairingly to the Earl of Dartmouth, Secretary of State for the Colonies, in London: "I have learnt from experience that the established Authority of any government in America, and the policy of Government at home, are both insufficient to restrain the Americans. . . . They acquire no attachment to Place; But wandering about Seems engrafted in their Nature; and it is a weakness incident to it, that they Should for ever immagine the Lands further off, are Still Better than those upon which they are already settled."

Among the few mountaineers I knew well during the time we lived at Poor Fork, there was no one who did not possess innate intelligence and good common sense. Naturally, opportunities for formal education were limited. Nor is it to be denied that at times there was lawlessness. But lawlessness is characteristic of

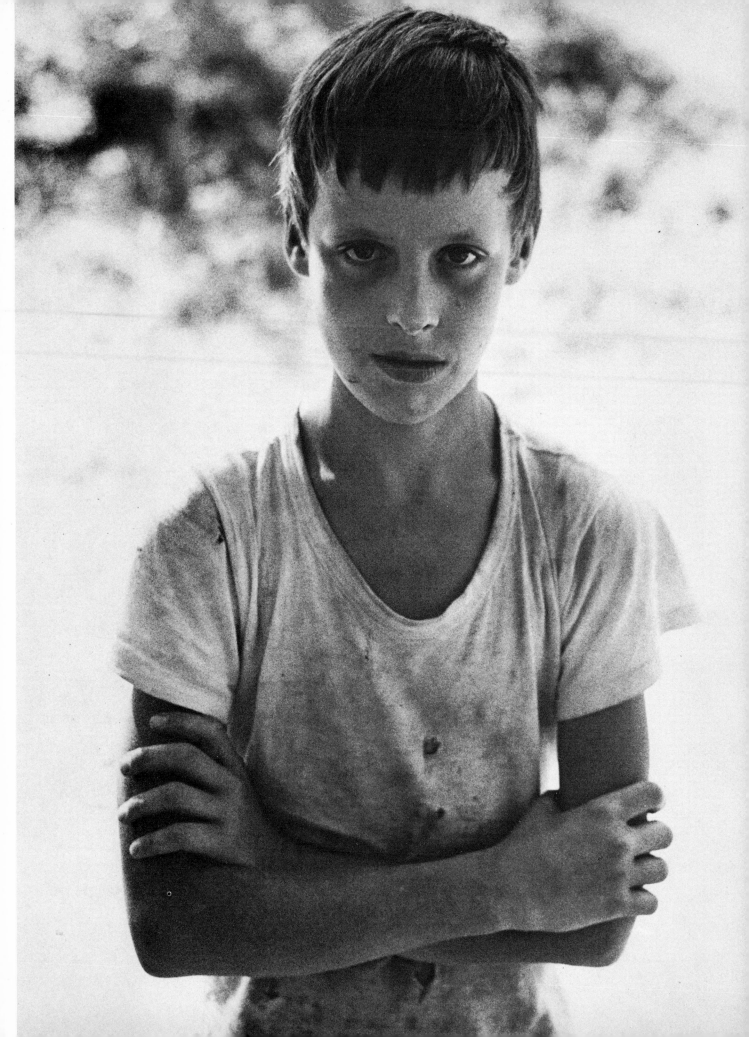

pioneer mountain areas in which, because of numerous hideouts, law enforcement is difficult.

Both my father and mother were teachers, and at one time my father served as a member of the Kentucky Textbook Commission. I suspect that both his formal education and Mother's ended at the eighth grade or perhaps earlier. That in a true sense they were educated, however, there was no doubt. Perhaps the finest heritage they passed on to us, their children, was the desire for an education.

Sometimes, as we sat about the fire, we sang old hymns, most of them with tunes peculiar to the mountains, such as "Amazing Grace," "When the Roll Is Called Up Yonder," and my favorite, "Jesus Born in Beth'ny." We children did not grow up on Appalachian mountain ballads so much in vogue now and so much sought after by collectors. Stella introduced us to ballads when she came home from the Presbyterian Academy with a head and a notebook full of them.

No evening before the fire was complete until my father had emptied his lap of little squatters and popped corn in a big wire popper over the hot coals. When we had finished eating the popcorn, we stumbled sleepily to our rooms, where we fell into our warm featherbeds and knew nothing more until morning.

In whatever season, the mountains that towered over us were glorious and majestic, and continually full of surprises. Spring came to them shyly and tenuously. In the beginning appeared the whitish flowers of the maples that the unknowing could easily mistake for young and tender leaves. Let the earth be treated to a few days of warm sunshine, and the mountainsides unfurled in every shade of green, from the delicate yellow-green of the tulip poplars to the reddish-green of the oaks. Splashed among these were the dark green of the pines and the shiny green of the holly.

Before leaves appeared on the trees, starting even before water from the melting snows had run down the steep mountainsides to swell the rivers, wild flowers had begun their seasonal procession across the mountains. In early March, if the winter had not been too long and cold, we could climb Broomsedge Hill and find spring beauties and blue-eyed grass, fragile

and dainty, coming out of the woods and running down the mountain to meet us. In our joy at finding them, we knelt and cupped them lovingly in our hands, and buried our noses in them.

At such times we could hear Father's voice reciting the lilting poetry from the Song of Solomon: "For, lo, the winter is past, the rain is over and gone; the flowers appear on the earth; the time of the singing of birds is come, and the voice of the turtle is heard in our land."

I wondered often about that turtle. I had never heard the voice of a turtle, though I had once listened eagerly as I trailed one when he crawled from one spot to another. And once I squatted a half hour over a turtle that had decided to remain just where he was, to hear any sound he might utter. Maybe he only whispered, I thought, and only the very wise, or the very old, or the very good could hear him. I had my honest doubts about his having a voice. But God had written the Bible, hadn't he? I could only conclude therefore that what the Bible said was not to be questioned. I felt cheated when I learned that the writer of the song was actually writing of a turtle dove.

Each April, on a Sunday afternoon, our family went up into the mountains in a picnic mood to observe a springtime ritual. Whenever my father decided the proper day had arrived, he shouldered an ax, my mother gave to each of us children a teaspoon, and off we went, up the mountain to a spot where grew a grove of black birch trees. Father looked over the grove carefully, chose a sapling for the sacrifice, and chopped it down. Then, with his ax, he pried off the smooth bark in squares and gave a square to each of us. We sat about on stumps or on fallen tree trunks, and with our spoons scraped the inside of the bark for the sap that was both sweet and spicy, like wintergreen. This was the best of all spring days.

When the season of riotous blooming was over, came the season of fruiting on the mountainsides. In the woods we gathered buckets full of wild huckleberries, and along fencerows even greater quantities of large and luscious blackberries. In the fall, there were pawpaws to pick and, after frost, juicy persimmons.

In September, though the days were sometimes sultry, the nights grew chill. Quietly, almost imperceptibly, the

mountains changed. Here a leaf on a sour gum tree turned red, there a leaf on a poplar turned gold, harbingers of glory to come. Then, October flamed across the steep mountainsides and deep into every hollow. There was one glory of the scarlet oak, and another glory of the bronzy beech, and another glory of the sweet gum, its star-shaped leaves a riot of color from pale gold to purple, outdone only by the saucy sassafras sprout which might boast no more than a dozen leaves, but each a different vivid hue.

As we had our springtime ritual, so we had also our autumn ritual. This always took place on a Saturday afternoon after the first hard frost, when all the children living along the river followed my father to the woods, each of us carrying a basket or a bucket, or wearing an apron that could be gathered up for carrying things. We were going chestnut-hunting, and the mood was gay, the chatter lively. When we arrived at a chestnut tree, my father climbed it and shook the branches one by one. Down peppered the rich brown chestnuts, freed by the frost from their prickly burs, while underneath the tree we greedily gathered them up for the winter.

Our celebration of Christmas in Appalachia was unlike any I have ever known elsewhere. No one gave or received gifts. No Christmas trees were trimmed and lighted. No carols were sung. Instead, on Christmas Eve when the èarth was stilled in darkness, we wrapped warmly against the brittle cold and gathered in our front yard, where Father shot Roman candles high above the barren trees against the starlit sky.

I sometimes think of our Appalachian Christmases and wonder what celebration could be more appropriate than to witness a sudden brillance flashing among the stars, and then to go to bed to think for a while on the mystery and majesty of it before drifting off to sleep.

The fall I was three, when the older children were getting ready to go to school one morning, Father, who for some reason was going across the mountain with them, said, "Get Becky ready, too."

"What for?" chorused my brother and sisters.

"She can go to school today," said Father.

Getting me ready became a family project. While Mother scrubbed my face and neck and ears, Cappie brought my other dress (as children we had only two dresses in a season), Stella combed my hair, and Will tied my shoes. Off we set, skirting Broomsedge Hill and crossing the mountain to the schoolhouse that stood on the other side of Clover Lick Creek. On the way, other children joined us, all of them sharing generously the excitement of my going to school.

There was one obstacle on the path to school about which I knew nothing. Encountering it, I was plunged into fear. A swinging bridge, built of barrel staves woven together with wire, spanned Clover Lick Creek, and it had to be crossed to reach the schoolhouse. Stout ropes stretched on either side of the bridge and fastened securely to trees served as guard rails, while short lengths of saplings nailed side by side to stringers formed a long ramp at each end of the bridge.

As the other children started up the ramp in long striding steps, I hung back in fear. I wanted to ask my father to carry me across. But pride at being allowed to go to school kept me from it. I must walk like the other children, like Clara, I told myself.

My father took my hand in his, and up the ramp we started. Our progress was slow, for I had to step on every sapling crosspiece, not with one foot only, but with both.

"We're getting there," encouraged my father.

I was high enough on the ramp so that when I looked down I could see, beneath me, bushes and saplings waving in the wind.

"Keep your eyes on the bridge," said Father.

Finally we arrived at the bridge, but keeping my footing while the bridge bounced and swayed under the footsteps of the other children was more difficult than climbing the first ramp. And, after the bridge, there was the other ramp to go down.

Finally we made it to the ground and continued the short distance to the schoolhouse. There my father deposited me, with or without the approval of the teacher, I don't know. Then he went on his way.

In the schoolhouse, Stella and her deskmate, Zerah Cornett, took charge of me. Seated between them, I was highly entertained all day by making marks and drawing pictures on Stella's slate, and looking at pictures in a geography book. When the first grade children were called to the front of the room, Stella sent me with them, to sit on the hard recitation bench, and to look and listen. A big chart standing in the front of the room was the "book" from which the children learned their lesson. The page serving as the lesson that day had on it the pictures of a cat. Underneath the picture were bold black marks—*c-a-t*—that, according to the teacher, said *cat*. I sensed there was something important about those marks. A cat could be three different kinds of creature, I thought: a cat, the picture of a cat, and *c-a-t*.

The reading classes were called to the recitation bench by turns the first periods of the morning. I sat quietly and with prickles on my arms as I listened to wonderful stories and fables and fairy tales and poetry. The prickles grew larger as I listened to Stella read *Robert of Lincoln*. Stella was never one to do anything halfheartedly. When she stood up straight before the class and read:

> Bob-o-*link*! Bob-o-*link*!
> *Spink*! Spank! Spink!

I forgot for a moment that I wasn't hearing real bobolinks calling and calling across the tall windblown grass on Broomsedge Hill.

I made one other discovery that day—as important as divining that printed symbols were a way of communication. All day, hidden as deeply as I could bury it, was the knowledge that the bridge had to be crossed on the way home, and that my father would not be along to hold my hand.

When school was out, most of the boys and girls made for the bridge with a whoop. Cappie, seeing my hesitation, took me by the hand and led me. When we reached the ascending ramp, Clara pranced by and started up the ramp, showing no fear whatever. For a minute I watched her as I clung to Cappie's hand. Then, quite ungratefully, I jerked my hand free and started up the ramp alone, stepping on every crosspiece, first with one foot, then with the other, but making progress.

At the bridge Cappie again offered aid, and again I spurned it. Clinging tightly to one of the guide ropes, I finally crossed the bridge and descended the ramp on the opposite side, backwards, as I would have climbed down a ladder, stepping on every crosspiece, first with one foot, then with the other. All the other children were a long way ahead of me when finally my feet touched safe earth. But what did that matter? In the act of crossing the bridge alone, I had become Somebody, Myself, I. Through the woods I ran till I caught up with the others. Proudly I walked along with them, now one of them.

At home the next day, it occurred to me that perhaps all the strange marks on the pages of the Louisville *Courier-Journal,* with which our walls were papered, also said words. Before this, our wallpaper had intrigued me, but only because my mother had pasted around the four walls of our living room, over the newspapers, a band of colored pages of fashionably dressed ladies taken one a month from *McCall's* magazine.

Now I neglected the fine ladies of *McCall's* and began to study the fine print of the *Courier-Journal*. Nothing made sense, because I could not find *c-a-t*. When Mother discovered what I was trying to do, she set out to help me learn the alphabet. While the older children were at school, she taught me both how to read and write the alphabet. Then followed simple words, *the* and *and* and *I* and *you, cow* and *dog, creek* and *river* and *mountain,* which I was set to looking for on the wallpaper and then to printing on my slate. Whenever my father was in the house, which in wintertime was often, he too helped me.

School always closed in December after a four-and-a-half- or a five-month session. Then Stella took over my "education." Through a combination of Stella's flattery, my own delight in new daily discoveries, and my eagerness to devour the wallpaper mentally, by spring I could read.

Every year, before the opening of school in August, my father saddled his horse, threw saddlebags across the saddle, said good-bye to all of us, and set out on a two-day journey over Big Black Mountain to Stonega, Virginia. This journey always took place the last week of July. The heyday of the year was when he returned with saddlebags bulging with new school

books for all of us who were in school, new tablets and pencils, new slates and slate pencils.

The summer after my fourth birthday, shortly after our noon meal on the day following Father's departure for Stonega, Clara and I took our stand on the front gate to watch for his return. We were warned many times during the afternoon by Mother that Father might not be home until dark. But we knew nothing of time, and back and forth we swung on the gate, and watched, and waited.

Almost overwhelming was the excitement when Father finally came in sight down the road. As he hitched the horse at the gate and lifted off the saddlebags, all of us children hurried to the porch to gather around while he placed in the outstretched hands of each of us new clean books smelling fresh and crisp. I had taken for granted that, having gone to school one day the fall before, and being now able to read, I should enter school as a first-grader. And I was not disappointed. Father laid in my outstretched hands a first reader, a book which I came to love as I have never loved another. No doubt Kentucky had a law stating at what age a child should enter school. No doubt, too, the Department of Education prescribed what books should be used in Kentucky schools. Little that was said and done in Frankfort affected us in our mountain fastness, however. It may be that Father simply bought what was available in the nearest or in the most accessible trading center. Or it may be that he bought what appealed to him as a former teacher and always a lover of good reading.

My first reader was filled with folk tales such as "Henny Penny," and "Chicken Licken," "The Three Little Pigs," and "Little Red Riding Hood." The other readers, too, for the early grades were filled with beloved tales—"Jack and the Beanstalk," "The Tar Baby," "Why the Sea is Salt," "Cinderella," "The Billy Goats Gruff," "The Ugly Duckling." The fifth reader contained old Norse myths, while the sixth was a miscellaneous collection of stories and poems.

I sat entranced every morning as the pupils of one class after another recited their reading lessons. I suffered in anguish at the reading of "The Ugly Duckling" and came to imagine myself something of an ugly duckling since whatever was to be done, in school or

at home, Clara could do better than I. When the fifth grade was reading the lesson called "Balder Is Dead," I laid my head on the desk and sobbed.

Books? There were many school books in our house. Except for those, we had only the Bible. This my father read often, and much of it he knew by heart and quoted to us on appropriate occasions. "Go to the ant, thou sluggard; consider his ways and be wise." "In his hand are the deep places of the earth: the strength of the hills is his also." I have always been grateful that the school books Father chose provided the kind of reading to inspire us, to stretch our minds, to exercise our imaginations.

During the summer after I had finished the first grade, I sensed that something unusual was afoot in our household. I overheard snatches of conversation between my father and my mother—conversation about level land, about the lawlessness and killing in the mountains (a young man had just been killed at a box supper held in our schoolhouse), about the education of us children. Often Father lectured us on getting an education. "What you carry in your head, nobody can take from you," he said to us many times.

One day my father rode away on his horse across Big Black Mountain to a destination unnamed to us children, and the reason therefor unexplained. After three days he returned, his journey still unexplained, either by him or by my mother.

In a few days, he set out again as mysteriously as before. When at last he came home, he had news for us. He had sold his river-bottom farm on the Poor Fork and had bought another in Carter's Valley across the mountains in eastern Tennessee. Carter's Valley was a mighty pretty place, he said. We would be moving as soon as we could dispose of our furniture, which was too cumbersome to haul across Big Black.

It was plain to see that Father was elated over his new farm, and that Mother shared the elation, even though moving meant leaving behind her most beloved possession—the little organ she had bought before her marriage with the meager savings from her salary as a school teacher. It was arranged, however, that she might take her sewing machine, the one other possession, also bought with her own savings, which had made up her

wedding "dowry." We would go across Big Black in a wagon, Father said, to Big Stone Gap, Virginia, where we would take a train to Gate City. From there we would take a hack—an open, multiseated conveyance with a fringe around the top—to our farm in Carter's Valley.

All my waking hours I thought of nothing but the journey. We children had never crossed Big Black Mountain. None of us had ever seen a train. What was a train like?

The last night in Poor Fork we were all promised we might spend the night with whatever friend we chose. I chose to spend the night with Jim and Cassie Huff. Jim and Cassie at that time had no little children of their own—later they adopted a daughter. So for one night at least I received more than my due of attention. A young man named Pres Hall was there also. Pres lived somewhere in the neighborhood, but who he was and what he did I never knew. I thought he existed to make children happy.

Among other good things, Cassie had fresh honey and hot biscuits for supper. I was seated beside Pres at the table. As soon as he saw I was finishing one biscuit with honey, he put another biscuit and more honey on my plate. I hadn't read my Shakespeare then and didn't know to say, "Hold, enough!" As long as Pres put hot biscuits and honey on my plate, I thought I had to eat them, even though I felt like a goose stuffed for a Christmas feast. Finally, seeing I was paling, Cassie came to my rescue and suggested to Pres that I had eaten quite enough.

The next morning all of us returned home and climbed into the waiting wagon, father clucked to the horses, slapped their rumps with the reins, and we were off down the road toward the fording place in the Poor Fork River.

In my excitement, I never once looked back.

Not until long afterward did I realize what we had left behind. Most important were the people, unhurried, kind, independent, determined, with big families and close and loyal family ties. Money was of no importance in the life of anyone I knew. If a man was sick, womenfolks helped nurse him to health, while the menfolks tended to his planting, his plowing, his harvesting. A man was judged by what

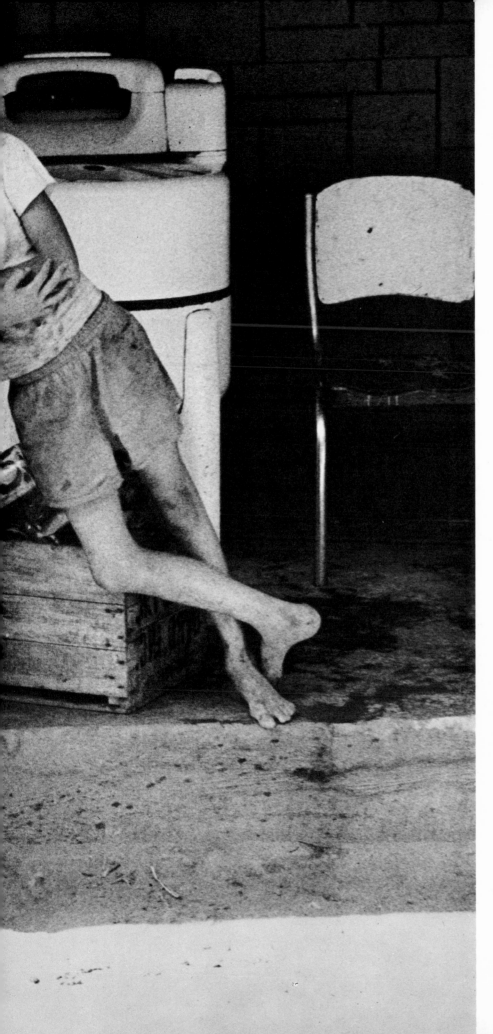

he was, never by what he had. Doors in the houses of my Appalachia were never locked against friend or stranger. The people found their pleasures in the simple things of life. They possessed a kind of profound wisdom, characteristic of those who live close to Nature, who walk in step with Nature's rhythm, and who depend on Nature for life itself.

The mountains, too, we left behind—the undefiled mountains to which my people could lift up their eyes and gather strength, and calmness of spirit, and courage to face what life demanded of them. The wholeness of the mountains and the wholeness of the people were one.

Before we left, however, there had been ominous signs of changes to come. The last winter we lived at Poor Fork, when the melting snows were swelling the river, we had heard high on Pine Mountain the sound of many axes and crosscut saws, and, more often than was required for the needs of my people, the crashing of giant trees to the earth. I had sat often on the stairs by the kitchen window and watched loggers snake immense logs to the top of the Dump, a big bald-faced rock across the river from the Huffs' house, and roll them down into the river to start them on their way to sawmills somewhere along the Cumberland. Also we had heard rumors that cash money jingled in the pockets of some mountaineer up the river who had sold a patch of land to an outlander.

Years later when I went back to Poor Fork, I found other faces, other names, other standards by which people lived. While I was away, tragedy had struck at my Appalachia, tragedy dark, stark, and irreversible.

Yesterday

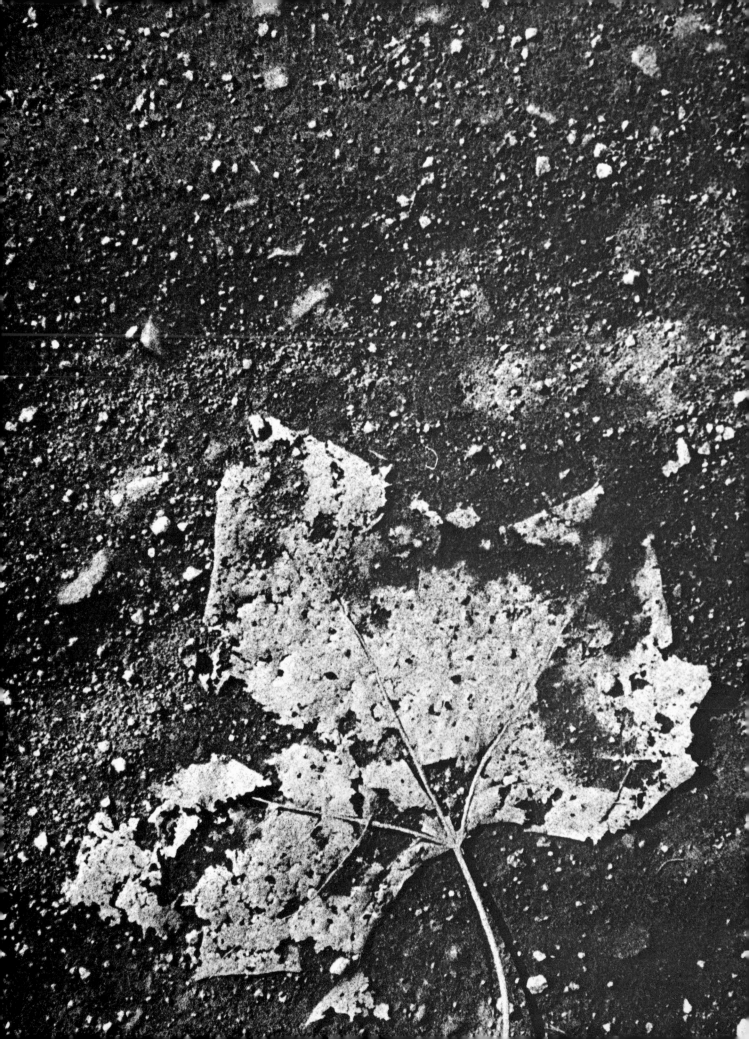

In 1893, Colonel M. H. Crump of Bowling Green, Kentucky, was commissioned to arrange and display the Kentucky Mineral Exhibit at the World's Columbian Exposition held in Chicago. At the end of the exposition, he made an enthusiastic report to the Inspector of Mines.

"The exhibit," reported Colonel Crump "attracted great attention, and was excelled by no state in the Union, and was only equalled by West Virginia in its quality and excellence . . . more than 30 awards, carrying medals and diplomas, setting forth the various qualities of the coal, were received. . . . In cannel coal it far exceeded any other state. . . . No less than 50 papers, from Maine to California, reproduced the . . . description. Not less than 400,000 visitors passed under the arch and inspected, more or less critically, the exhibit; of these, more than 75,000 left their names upon the register. . . ."

At the time Colonel Crump made his report, coal for commercial uses was being mined in twenty-eight Kentucky counties. The combined output of these counties for 1893 was 3,007,179 tons. Hopkins, Ohio, and Muhlenberg counties in western Kentucky and Whitley County on the edge of the Cumberland Plateau led all other counties in production because of their ready access to rivers on which coal companies, in the absence of railroads, depended for transportation. Little coal for commercial uses was then mined in the Appalachians.

About the time I was born and for a few years thereafter, exciting information now and then passed by word of mouth from neighbor to neighbor: "One of them city fellers is around, I hear." Everyone, immediately on hearing the word, knew what the city fellow looked like and what his business was. He was an agent, doubtless for one of the 400,000 who had inspected Colonel Crump's exhibit. The agent came from somewhere far away over the rim of the mountains; no one knew exactly where, nor did it matter. That he was an outlander was evident from the store-bought clothes he wore, from the fine language he spoke, and from the fancy manners to which he seemed to be born. Yet he was not above entering a mountaineer's cabin, sitting down by the fire, and chatting with the man of the house while the wife and the brood of children looked on and listened, silent and curious. At mealtime he was

invited to eat with the family, which he did with rare grace, not forgetting to compliment the wife on her delicious corn pone and shucky beans, saying they were certainly the best he had ever eaten.

After the meal, with the amenities out of the way, he returned to the fireside, ready to talk business. He was just out looking over the land, he told the mountaineer casually. He had in mind buying up some of it, if the price was right. Well, not the land, he explained, only rights to the timber on the land or to the coal and other minerals below the surface of the land. The mountaineer would continue sole ownership of the surface. The surface would be exclusively his. He would continue to live on his acres and to plant and harvest his crops as he had done in the past, the only difference now being that he would have some cash money in his pocket.

Under the spell of the outlander's affability and charm, the mountaineer, accustomed to barter trading only, saw sudden visions of new shoes all around for his children, or a new rifle, or a new roof on his cabin to replace the leaky one, or maybe an entirely new house, or perhaps even a level bluegrass farm on the other side of the mountains. Accordingly, he ordered his wife to draw the splint-bottomed chairs up to the table again, while the outlander took legal-size sheets out of his portfolio and set about explaining the terms of the proposed transaction.

On the lower slopes of the mountains grew thousands of stately tulip poplars, many of them one hundred and fifty feet tall, and burly white oaks five feet in diameter; higher on the mountainsides towered other oaks— red, black, and chestnut. Interspersed among these were hickories, buckeyes, basswoods, mountain and hard maples, black gums, ash, cedars, pines, hemlocks, and chestnuts, while hugging the banks of every stream giant sycamores flung wide their ghostly arms. Thousands of these trees were bought by agents of logging companies at forty to sixty-five cents a tree.

Mineral rights were often obtained by agents of coal corporations at the paltry sum of fifty cents an acre, though as the mountaineers grew wise to the value of coal the prices rose, in some cases of sharp bargaining, to five dollars an acre. In exchange for the

pittance they were paying, the agents were obtaining in a single acre from fifteen to twenty thousand tons of easily mined coal, plus thousands of tons of less accessible coal, plus all other mineral properties—gas, oil, slate, iron—that might be found under the surface of the earth.

In the deed books shelved in Appalachian courthouses are to be found many a "long-form" or "broad-form" deed drawn up by an affable agent and signed by him as representative of the party of the second part, and by a mountaineer and his wife as party of the first part. Under the spotlight turned on Appalachia today, these deeds make astounding reading.

Part of a six-page long-form deed recorded in the courthouse at Whitesburg, Letcher County, Kentucky, reads as follows:

"Witnesseth; that said parties of the first part, in consideration of the sum of ($1.00) One dollar and other good and valuable considerations . . . do hereby bargain, sell, grant and convey unto the said Roberta Coal Company . . . party of the second part . . . all coal, minerals and mineral substances and products; all oils and gases; all salt and salt mineral waters; all fire and potters clay; all iron and iron ores; all stone; all slate; all ores and mines; and all subterranean substances and products, and all combinations of same, or any or all the same; situated, lying and being in, on or under the hereinafter described land, or that may hereafter be found thereon, therein or thereunder; and such of the standing timber thereupon as may, at the time of the use thereof, be, or by the party of the second part, its successors or assigns, be deemed necessary or convenient for mining purposes, or so deemed necessary or convenient for the exercise and enjoyment of any or all the property, rights and privileges herein bargained, sold, granted or conveyed including timber necessary for dams and railroads, or branch lines thereof, as may hereafter be constructed upon the said lands; and the exclusive rights-of-way for any and all railroads, tram roads, haul roads and other ways . . . and also the exclusive right to enter upon said land and drill thereupon for oil and gas, and to pump for and store the same upon said land, and remove, pipe and transport the

same therefrom, and to use and operate the said land surface thereof, and any and all parts thereof, including the right to use, divert, dam and pollute water courses thereon in any and every manner that may, by party of the second part, its successors or assigns, be deemed necessary or convenient for the full and free exercise and enjoyment of any and all the property, rights and privileges hereby bargained, sold, granted or conveyed . . . and the right to dump, store and leave upon said land any and all muck, bond, shale, water or other refuse . . . that may be excavated from mines . . .

And in the use and occupation of said land and surface thereof in any manner hereunder . . . said party of the second part, its successors and assigns, shall be free from, and it and they are hereby released from any and all liabilities or claim of damage to the said parties of the first part, their heirs, representatives and assigns, occasioned by or resulting directly or indirectly from such use or occupation, or the exercise of said rights or privileges, or any or all of them."

The only privilege retained by the mountaineer, but nowhere mentioned in the deed, was the obligation of himself, his heirs, and assigns to pay the taxes perpetually on his property, taxes being levied on surface land only, and none on whatsoever of riches that might be extracted from below the surface.

Not all of the transactions between corporation agents and mountaineers involved only the timber or mineral rights. Some of them involved immense tracts of mountain land bought outright at phenomenally low prices from mountaineers who had no way of knowing the true value of the property they were selling.

Streams for floating logs to market were plentiful and convenient in eastern Kentucky at the time timber rights were being bought up. Hundreds of mountaineers, balancing crosscut saws on their shoulders and carrying sharpened axes in their hands, went up on the mountainsides during the winter months to work for the new owners of the timber. Thousands of immense trees fell to their tools, oftentimes splintering and destroying other valuable trees in their mighty fall, the sound of which reverberated through the mountains. When the trees were shorn of their branches, the

trunks were snaked by oxen to the nearest dump or rollway. There they were piled up to wait for the melting snows and spring freshets to swell the streams that would carry them down to sawmills on the Cumberland and other large rivers.

To extract the coal from the mountains required extensive preparation. One important operation confronting the corporations that had now come into possession of untold wealth was the building of spurs to mountain railroads so that coal could be got to market. Other operations were the construction of tipples for loading the coal into railroad cars, the sawing of timbers for propping up the mine ceilings as the coal was removed, and the building of towns or camps for housing the miners.

So great was the sudden demand for eastern Kentucky coal, especially cannel coal, which contained much volatile matter, burned with a bright flame, and produced a negligible amount of ash, and so anxious were corporations to show quick profits that they imported additional labor— Negroes from the Deep South and immigrants from Europe—to work alongside the mountaineers. From daylight to dusk, these men with stout backs and strong arms sawed down trees and hauled the trunks by ox teams to nearby sawmills. The high whine of circular saws could be heard through the mountains as they sawed out hundreds of thousands of crossties for the railroads and timbers for the mines, as well as lumber for the towns.

While the railroads were being extended, surveyors and engineers were on the mountainsides determining the proper places for opening up mines, for locating necessary machinery, and for building the tall tipples, many of which, swaybacked and grayed by weather, can be seen today as relics of the beginning of a new and treacherous way of life for the mountaineers.

Many towns for miners were built by the coal companies, because most mines were a considerable distance from any established towns and in hitherto wilderness land. Apart from the other houses, "nigger towns" were built by the companies for the Negro miners and their families.

Prior to and during World War I, my sister Cappie worked as secretary to the presidents of three coal-mining

corporations: in Jenkins, Letcher County, eastern Kentucky; in Sturgis, Union County, western Kentucky; and in Colver, Cambria County, Pennsylvania. In the thirties, before the outbreak of World War II, my sister Alma taught in high schools of two West Virginia mining towns. She married an electrician employed by a mining company in West Virginia and continued to live in that state for a while. Through them I heard many stories about the manner in which Southern Appalachian coal companies operated.

Coal companies differed greatly in their attitudes toward miners. Some paid their miners fair wages and were solicitous of their welfare. Others hired their miners at the lowest possible wages, drove them at their labor, and gave little thought to their welfare. Many shortweighted their miners and held out as long as they could against demands for checkweighmen of the miners' choice to guarantee that the coal dug was honestly weighed and that each miner was given full credit for the coal he dug. In some mines, scales were so manipulated that one hundred pounds of coal registered only eighty pounds.

Some mining towns were substantially built. Houses were painted and surrounded with green lawns enclosed by whitewashed picket fences. Gates opened onto concrete walks. Recreation halls, hospitals, and attractively furnished clubhouses where unmarried employees could live distinguished these towns from most coal towns.

The usual mining town, hurriedly thrown together by companies anxious to show quick profits during the boom years of coal mining, presented a dismal aspect—jerry-built unpainted shacks hammered together of unseasoned lumber, many of them on stilts, and lined up in rows in a narrow valley near a coal tipple. One unshaded light bulb hung from the ceiling of each of three tiny rooms; in very few houses was there running water or such a luxury as a flush toilet.

With few exceptions, the coal companies demanded that their miners live in company-owned shacks assigned to them. The rent deducted from a miner's monthly wages soon paid for the building of his shack.

Common to every coal-mining town was a commissary, an institution that

reached into the lives of all miners, black, native white, and foreign-born alike. The commissary was the "storehouse," as the mountaineer called it, where he could find any of the necessities of life plus many luxuries he didn't need and couldn't afford.

No miner was required to buy at the commissary. It was there for his convenience. He was paid in legal tender at the end of each month, and he was free to spend his money where and for whatever he pleased. But because the commissary was the store most convenient to him and his family, he quickly fell into the habit of doing his trading—and his gossiping—there.

The manager of the commissary was more sales-conscious than our Poor Fork merchants, Jim Huff and Will Cornett. He arranged his wares attractively to tempt the miner's wife as well as the miner. And he marked his items consistently higher— sometimes as much as 25 percent higher—than the same items in noncompany stores.

With so many attractively displayed items to which the mountaineer miner and his wife were not accustomed, and with an income higher than they had known before, it was natural that they were lured into the commissary many times to look at items they wanted.

They found their shopping sprees made easy and painless through the use of scrip, metal discs and paper available in the same denominations as legal tender of twenty dollars and less. The scrip was issued by the coal company and was obtainable from the commissary in any amount not greater than the wages due the miner on the date of asking. Some companies, sensitive to the needs of the many foreign-born working in the mines, issued books of scrip with directions for use printed on the covers in Polish, German, Spanish, and Italian, in addition to English.

The scrip was not acceptable at any store other than the commissary.

When a handout of scrip was exhausted, more could be had, again in any amount not greater than that due the miner on the date of asking. Many miners ended the month with their entire wages already spent in scrip at the commissary. And back on the commissary they had to go again to tide them over still another month.

Because a post office was needed in each mining town, the coal company was generous in its offer to lease to the Postmaster General space in the commissary for the handling of mail. The rent of this space not only helped retire the cost of the building, but it lured customers into the commissary every day. In some of the larger towns boasting three or four commissaries, each commissary obligingly served its section of town with a post office.

Some coal-producing states passed a law requiring the commissary to make change for the miner in legal tender if he requested it. No company advertised this, and apparently no miner knew of it.

In most mining towns, the schoolhouse was built by the coal company and leased to the county board of education for a sum sufficient in a few years to pay for the building. Often, Negro children went without schooling.

The company delivered coal to the miner's shack and provided his electricity, the cost of both of which it deducted from his monthly wage. It provided him with water—if his house was equipped with plumbing—and withheld from his pay envelope the amount of his water bill. It withheld from his monthly wage also an amount to cover the expenses of himself and his family for minor ills treated by the company doctor (if the doctor could be persuaded to come in answer to a call). As a final and touching rite of paternalism, the company withheld from the miner's wages an amount to insure burial by a mortician under contract to the company.

No official count was kept of the miners whose lives were instantly snuffed out by naked cables hung from tunnel roofs, by the falling of huge slabs of slate overhead, and by explosions inside the mines. In Kentucky, the law required the company to carry insurance on each miner. If a miner was totally disabled, he received $4,400, prescribed by the state legislature as an equitable sum. If he was killed outright, his widow received $4,000, paid to her in monthly driblets over a period of years. Then, in accordance with the contract the miner had signed with the company, instead of being given a month's notice to vacate the shack the family occupied, the miner and his family (if he was injured) or his widow and his children (if he was killed) had to vacate the shack at once so that an

able-bodied miner could move in. Where did they go with their poor and shabby belongings piled outside the door? Where could they go but back into the mountains to the house of some relative who crowded them in?

In many coal-producing counties, particularly those in eastern Kentucky and West Virginia, mining quickly became the sole important source of revenue, and on it almost every resident soon depended directly or indirectly. Thousands of native mountaineers exchanged subsistence farming and the sunlight of their cleared mountainside acres for cash money and the perpetual pitch darkness of a mine. People engaged in businesses in already-established towns near mines soon found that their profits depended almost entirely on the coal industry.

As coal corporations quickly uprooted a people and changed their economic patterns and standards of living, so, too, they quickly introduced new political patterns undreamed of among those who voted with deadly loyalty Republican or Democratic in an earlier day at Poor Fork.

From county-wide economic dependence on the coal industry to political takeover by the coal companies was but one short step. Some of the larger coal towns sought and were granted their own charters. In such towns, the mayor, members of the city council, school trustees, policemen, and firemen were chosen, and their salaries were set, by the company officials—who also determined and controlled the revenues.

Though coal companies might enter into cutthroat competition with each other in business, in politics they were amiable partners. If several companies operated in a county, their managers met in the office of one of the companies, usually one located in the county seat, and there agreed on nominees for county school superintendent, county judge, tax commissioner, and so on to the end of the ballot, and never mind the political affiliation of any nominee. What was important was that, being subservient to the companies, he should dance to whatever tune they piped. Having chosen the "right" men to run for offices, the companies then instructed their employees how to vote.

One way in which the political hold of the companies was extended beyond

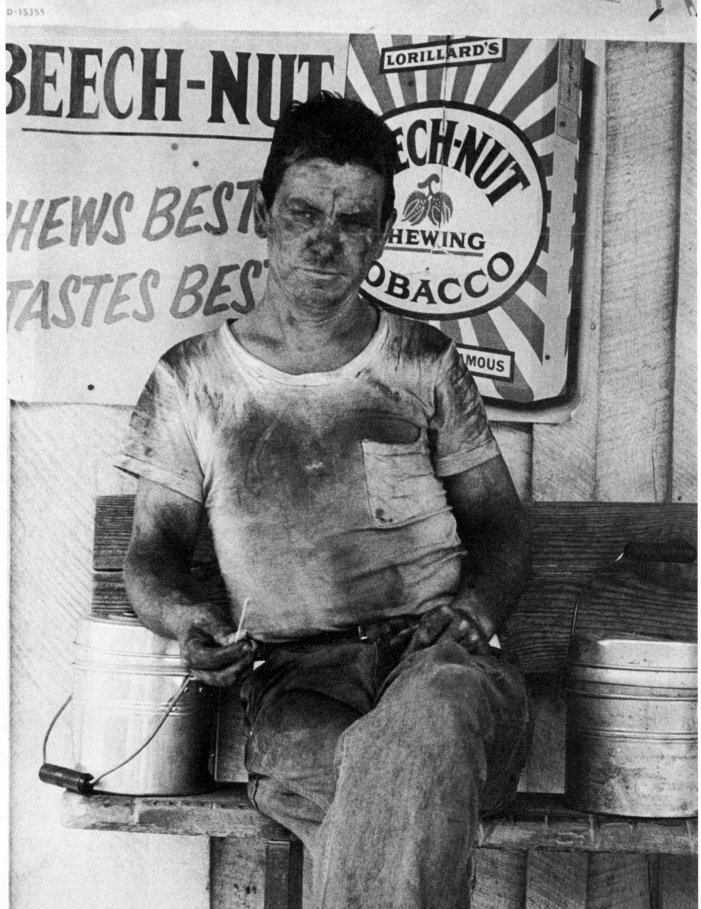

their employees and into the communities is illustrated by an experience of my sister Alma. During the depression, Alma was teaching in West Virginia when, shortly before an election day, she received notice to attend a faculty meeting called by the county superintendent of schools. At the meeting, the superintendent, who owed his job to a local coal company, instructed all of the teachers to contribute to the campaign fund of the political party of which he was a member. Alma protested. She said that her salary was so small that she could make no contribution. Her contract was not renewed.

The most insidious practice of the company-controlled officials was that, having taken oath of office to perform their duties according to law without fear or favor, they levied taxes according to company instructions. Through these officials, the coal companies kept taxes on all of their mining properties extremely low. On coal itself, the companies operating in Kentucky paid no tax. They have always been able to prevent imposition of a severance tax on this immense source of wealth—since the days of extensive lumbering the only considerable source of wealth of the mountain counties.

Eastern Kentucky counties, through their cheap, tax-free coal, almost all of it shipped out of the area, have for over half a century been subsidizing industry in other parts of the United States.

With the principal source of wealth of the area tax-free, revenue from other sources has been inadequate to provide the public services necessary to the welfare of the counties. As a consequence, east Kentuckians have put up with twisting, pocked roads cheaply built and poorly maintained by the counties, dilapidated schoolhouses, often poorly trained and always inadequately paid teachers, and few public libraries. These inadequacies have not been compensated for by boxes and barrels of cast-off clothing shipped from distant places by persons of good intent, possibly including stockholders in corporations perpetuating the existing inequitable tax system.

Though the coal industry in eastern Kentucky flourished from the day the first gondola loaded with "black gold" rumbled down a newly built spur on its way to market, it required World War I to make it Big Business. In 1915 the United States was receiving from the European Allies frantic appeals for more and more munitions. As orders for coal to produce these munitions piled up on company desks, they created a sudden and precipitous rise in the bidding for miners and in the price of coal. The companies tempted with promises of ready cash, and plenty of it, any able-bodied man they could find to enter the mines and dig—native mountaineer, foreign-born, or Negro. In their haste, they did not bother to ask him if he knew what all the shooting was about.

Into this runaway situation stepped the Federal Fuel Administration, which set the price of soft coal at $2.58 a ton, a price sufficient at that time to show a profit to any reasonably well-run mine.

When the War ended, price restrictions were lifted. With coal still in great demand, prices suddenly skyrocketed to $10 a ton at the mine, then to $14 a ton and, when transported oceanside, to $25 a ton. Almost anybody who could get a toehold on this source of sudden wealth left behind his other interests and joined the coal-crazy masses. Anything black, whether pure coal or coal that was half slate, could find a buyer. Miners sometimes earned fifty dollars a day—and easily parted with it for coveted items they found in the commissary or ordered from door-to-door salesmen who had quickly discovered that the company-owned towns were ripe for picking. From these salesmen the miners bought electric irons, victrolas, washing machines, carpet sweepers, Bibles, silk shirts (which they sometimes wore into the mines), and even automobiles. Many of the automobiles, driven with customary mountaineer daring on roads that were narrow, twisting, and shoulderless, ended their own and their owners' careers part way down some steep mountainside.

The interaction of war and coal follows a definite pattern of bang, boom, bust. After the great boom came the bust of 1920. Orders for coal dropped sharply. As the coal companies began laying off some miners and reducing the wages of all, recruiters for the United Mine Workers quietly arrived in the eastern Kentucky company-owned coal towns and in the coal camps on the edges of previously established towns.

News of the presence of a union recruiter in a coal town spread as quickly as the word had spread two decades earlier when a city fellow passed through the mountains buying up mineral rights. If a miner was suspected by company officials of having joined the union, he was immediately notified of the loss of his job and evicted from his shack, and his name was added to the blacklist that was circulated among all operators. Lured by the promise of higher wages plus other benefits, a few miners at a time stealthily joined the union.

It is something of an enigma that the United Mine Workers were successful in recruiting for membership in the union thousands of mountain men who by nature were not joiners. "You mind your own business!" we children used to snap if we thought some brother or sister was interfering with or prying into something that was no concern of his. Children, of course, learned this admonition from their elders. Mountain men often employed it. A mountaineer who was particularly hotheaded shot first and admonished later.

As the clouds of depression grew darker, fly-by-night coal companies died by the dozens. The well-established companies, following sounder financial practices, continued to exist but had to cut back operations. Great numbers of miners were summarily dismissed. Some went back "home" to raise a crop on their long untended acres and blink their eyes at the blinding sunlight. Others bummed their way to a place they called Dee-troit, where they found work with an automobile manufacturer, or became floaters and stood in breadlines. Still others, having no place to go, or no way to get there, stayed on in the coal towns and camps, where they congregated in groups to squat on the ground and whittle, to grumble, and to vent their distrust and growing hatred of the operators.

During the long period of cutthroat competition that followed the bust, operators everywhere in the industry employed the same tactics—underbidding on contracts by paring miners' wages.

In 1924, the United Mine Workers forced an agreement with the operators of one mine to guarantee its miners a minimum wage of $7 per day. The operators who had so far managed to keep free of the UMW took advantage of this situation to undercut the unionized mine price by paring

their own miners' wages still more. At this point, the miners realized that in the hands of the operators they were mere pawns. Miner after miner laid down his tools, walked out of the mines, and openly joined the union. Small wildcat strikes followed each other in waves.

Ranged on the side of the operators were police, armed with machine guns, and dozens of men, "deputized" and armed by the sheriff, roving the streets to help keep down trouble. These the miners referred to as "the law." In some strikes, brutal thugs from Chicago and other cities were imported as strikebreakers. On the side of the miners was only the UMW, which up to this point had not called a strike in the area.

As the country lowered itself into the Great Depression that followed the stock market crash of 1929, miners' wages in eastern Kentucky slid to one dollar a day or even below, while work for each miner still employed was reduced to a few days a month. The case cards of Red Cross workers in Harlan County reveal the resulting deprivation common among miners' families throughout the coal fields. A six-day report of one family living on two meals a day may be accepted as fairly typical. Breakfast: beans, three mornings; potatoes, one morning; gravy and apples, one morning; syrup, one morning. Supper: beans, four evenings; beans and bread, one evening; potatoes, one evening. Pellagra cases were numerous in all coal towns. In one Harlan County coal town, children died at the rate of seven per week of bloody flux.

In 1931, at the depth of the depression, about eleven thousand organized Harlan County miners appealed to the UMW to call a strike.

The union considered a strike at that time folly. It knew that the few coal companies still operating could scrape up scarcely enough contracts to continue in business. Many operators faced bankruptcy and were in almost as much distress as the miners. Several companies closed their mines for good. One owner turned over his mine to his miners, who were given the privilege of sharing in all earnings. The mine netted a profit of thirty cents a day per miner.

The Harlan County miners, goaded beyond endurance by hunger and disease in their families, struck without

benefit of sanction by the union. The UMW termed the strike a wildcat and refused to support it. Immediately the Red Cross, making a fine distinction between a national calamity and a labor difficulty, packed up and left the county.

The miners quickly lost faith in the UMW and turned to the National Miners Union, whose recruiters had arrived on the chaotic scene and were waiting with soup kitchens to feed the starving miners and their families, clothes to cover their half-naked bodies, and copies of *The Daily Worker* to distribute among them.

Widespread suspicion that the NMU was a Communist organization served as a bugle call for all good men to come to the aid of the great financial and industrial interests represented by the coal companies. Elected officials, bankers, grocers, editors, lawyers, and police, as well as religious groups and charitable institutions committed to serving the poor and the destitute—all desirous of standing well with vested interests that in one stroke could make them or undo them—either allied themselves against the miners or kept silent.

On May 5, 1931, the "Battle of Evarts" was fought between a carload of armed deputies and a few miners who had brought their shotguns, squirrel rifles, and pistols out of hiding and started out singly toward Evarts, not far from Harlan. The deputies, driving along the road, saw the armed miners, stopped their car, and got out. The battle was on. When the shooting was over, the bodies of at least three deputies and one miner lay lifeless in the dusty bushes beside the road. According to one report, twelve men lay dead.

A brief period of quiet followed the Battle of Evarts. Then, in June, Harlan County suddenly flamed across the front page of every big newspaper in the country as soup kitchens were dynamited, murders, never solved, were committed, and miners' shacks were ransacked without warrant by plainclothesmen claiming to be deputized by the sheriff. Every miner in whose shack copies of *The Daily Worker* were found was thrown into jail. Reporters who had been sent hurrying into the county were picked up at night, pushed into cars, and transported to Cumberland Gap, where, over the state line in

Tennessee, they were dragged out of the cars and beaten. Some were shoved over the edge of the road and down the mountainside. One reporter was shot in the leg as he tried to make his escape.

Onto this scene came Theodore Dreiser, author, representing the National Committee for the Defense of Political Prisoners, an organization of which he was the chairman. He hoped to interest nationally known persons of influence in government, industry, law, business, newspaper publishing, colleges, and churches in the plight of the Harlan County miners. Accordingly he sent a telegram to eighteen such persons, several of them in the Appalachian area. In the telegram, he pointed out the misery of the strikers and their families, the breakdown of law and order, and the disregard for free speech and free assembly. He asked the persons he addressed to accompany him to Harlan to make free and open inquiry on behalf of the miners. One of the eighteen, Bruce Crawford, publisher of *Crawford's Weekly* in Norton, Virginia, accepted Dreiser's invitation. Two did not reply. The others gave various reasons for their inability to become involved— reasons reminiscent of other well-known excuses: "I have bought a piece of ground, and I must needs go and see it: I pray thee have me excused." "I have bought five yoke of oxen, and I go to prove them: I pray thee have me excused." "I have married a wife, and therefore I cannot come."

Other persons less well-known in the area joined Dreiser and with him proceeded to Pineville, the county seat of Bell County, lying next to Harlan. Pineville was selected because officials of the National Miners Union had advised it would be safer than Harlan for interviewing the miners. Although Dreiser had obtained the promise of protection from the officers of the law, he and his co-workers soon discovered they were being constantly followed and spied on by the same officers. He therefore moved the hearings to Harlan and in the Lewallen Hotel heard testimony by miner after miner of daily harassment by "the law," of jailings and floggings, and the raiding of miners' shacks without warrant.

Finally, in Pineville, where Dreiser had continued to live, a resident known as a "local wit" trumped up a charge of

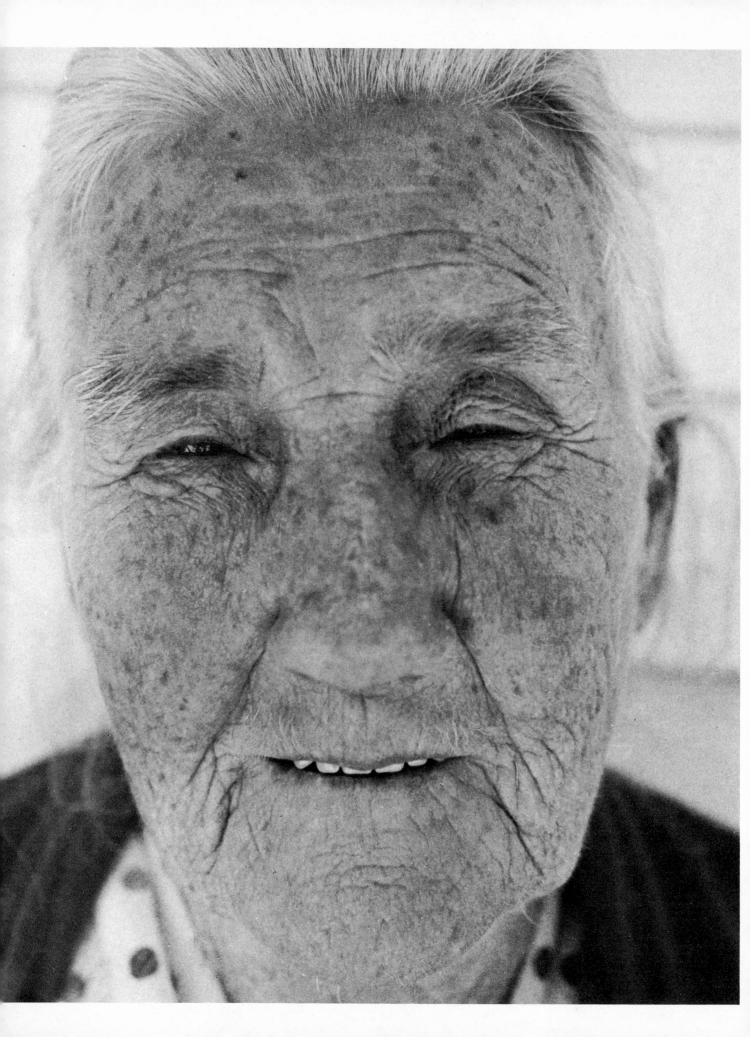

adultery against him, and the hearings came to a quick end. Embittered and discouraged, Dreiser shook the dust of eastern Kentucky off his clothes and went home to make a report to his organization. But his interest in the welfare of the miners of Harlan County did not cease. He made their welfare the center of his concern when he appealed for a Congressional hearing on his findings in Harlan County. And his life was testimony to his belief in freedom of speech and assembly, and in justice before the law.

His spirit might have been refreshed had he heard a sermon delivered by the Reverend L. C. Kelly in the First Baptist Church of Pineville soon after his departure.

"Through defending the law by violence, we break down the spirit of the law," declared Mr. Kelly. "The deadliest, dirtiest, darkest, meanest menace that confronts our land today is the disposition of every man to be a law unto himself. The alternative is the Christian way—Serpent wisdom and the guilelessness of a dove. Take, for instance, the organized miners and the organized coal operators. Suppose they could form a mutual cooperative Miners Union, where both sides could meet and frankly face the problems one sided, not two-sided. Let them together agree to put a price on mined coal that will pay the operator a just income on his investment, and a wage that will enable the coal loader to have a living wage, and the consumer to have a fire. . . . If leaders of Christian thought had stood for this all the years in these mountains, instead of meeting every exigency with the spirit of the flesh, we would have had a new day."*

Mr. Kelly's enlightened words fell on unlistening ears.

Having gotten rid of Dreiser, officers of the law in Pineville and Harlan proceeded to get rid in short order of other "meddlers" who followed. Some they chauffeured to Cumberland Gap, beat up, and pushed over the mountainside. Others they met at the county line and turned back. Still others, judged too innocent to leave the bus in which they arrived, they escorted out of the state. The "meddlers" included a group of distinguished authors headed by Waldo Frank; a delegation representing the American Civil Liberties Union; busloads of university students out to study sociology, and a

group of students arriving with the announced intention of testing freedom of speech. These last they tied to trees and whipped.

While these events were in progress, several miners and lay preachers were sent by the National Miners Union to cities in the North to be "educated." The mountaineers among the "students," instead of being converted by the so-called education, were horrified to the bone. These rock-ribbed fundamentalists were openly scandalized by the Communist assertion that there is no God, no Heaven, no Hell, no Hereafter—nothing to which a man in his earthly sufferings can look as a final reward. The return of these "students" and the stories they told in horror did more to break the back of the National Miners Union in Harlan County than anything else.

Early in the winter of 1931, President Hoover called to the White House for consultation a group of Quakers from the American Friends Service Committee in Philadelphia. Many of these had helped Mr. Hoover in his postwar task of feeding Europe's hungry millions. He now asked them to go into the Appalachian coal fields and do what they could to relieve the distress of the suffering miners. They accepted the challenge. They worked in thirty-eight counties, including Harlan and Bell, usually a Swarthmore and a Haverford student serving with an older person experienced in relief work. At first they were looked on suspiciously and spied on to see if they had come into the area to meddle. Quietly the Quakers went about ministering to the sick and hungry, distributing from outside relief agencies clothing and food for the miners and their families, yet speaking no word of evil against operators, against elected officials, against anyone. During the winter they fed two thousand children. In June of 1932, when the worst of the trouble seemed over, they went away as quietly as they had come, leaving coal operators, coal miners, and the rest of the populace sobered and wondering.

Harlan County, by virtue of the amount of blood shed during the desperate struggle, unintentionally took from Breathitt County its uncoveted title. Henceforth it was known as Bloody Harlan.

*Malcolm Ross, *Machine Age in the Hills* (New York, The Macmillan Company, 1933).

On a summer Sunday morning in 1938 in Harrodsburg, Kentucky, where I had been doing historical research, I glanced idly at the eastern section of a road map of Kentucky.

"Poor Fork!" I thought. "While I'm so near, why not go back to Poor Fork?"

Since I did not need to hurry home, I would go to see the place of my birth and early childhood.

Remembering vividly that other summer morning when our family had set out so blithely across Big Black Mountain, I searched the map for Poor Fork, but in vain. Never mind, I decided recklessly. It had to be there, and it was time I went back.

At the bus station, when I asked for a ticket to Poor Fork, the agent eyed me quizzically between the bars of the window separating us.

"Poor Fork, ma'am? Poor Fork's gone," he said. "Been gone a long time."

"Where did it go?" I asked.

"You ever been there?"

"Once." Then, to keep him from saying it, I added, "A long time ago."

"Well," he said, "if you're still a thinkin' of it as Poor Fork, you're in for a shock when you see it. Gone up in the world. Got a railroad through there and ever'thing. Changed its name to Cumberland. Them big coal mines in Harlan County, they've changed ever'thing. Anyway, can't sell you a ticket to Cumberland. Bus don't go there. Can sell you a ticket to Harlan."

Harlan! The word itself frightened me. I could think nothing good of Harlan. I had never even been there, I recalled. Moreover, so many years had passed since we had moved away from Harlan County that I wasn't sure who of my relatives, if any (they would be on my mother's side) still lived there.

"You want a ticket to Harlan?" the agent prodded me.

"All right," I said, feeling this trip was not turning out to be the carefree adventure I had thought I was planning, "give me a ticket to Harlan."

The bus had no sooner started rolling between the pampered, undulating fields around Harrodsburg than my mind began reviewing all I knew about the trouble in the Harlan County coal fields.

Miles later, as the bus labored up steep

slopes into the high mountains, I peered out the window. There stood the massive ranges, majestic and ongoing, dressed in the dark lusterless green of midsummer. Were the trees thinner on the high slopes? Some slopes, I noticed, were almost denuded of large trees and were covered instead with scrubby second growth.

The rivers beside the highway seemed much narrower and shallower than I remembered them. They were muddy, too, though I remembered them as running clear and clean. I recalled the first time I had gone home from college and had found the town near which I then lived looking only half as big as I had remembered it, the streets much narrower, the houses not grand at all but quite ordinary. Could it be, I wondered, that childhood memories are always tinged with romance—that nothing looked at through mature eyes can ever equal in grandeur one's childhood impressions?

I looked out the bus window again. This time I looked especially for the tulip poplar trees. In my childhood I had always thought of the tulip poplars as being the most queenly of trees because they stood so erect and shapely among the gnarled oaks, the crooked wild cherry trees, and the tattered and sprawling sycamores. Even in late fall, when most of the leaves on the mountainside forest had fallen, the poplars were still etched in gold by the few remaining leaves outlining their graceful shapes. But something, I saw, had happened to the poplars. I was not imagining now. The tall poplars I had known were gone from the lower slopes. I knew the chestnut trees had died of a blight, but I had not heard that a blight had attacked the poplars. I was to learn that there are other blights than natural ones, and that no blight is so deadly as that conceived in the calloused human mind.

My spirits were steadily sinking when the driver pulled up to a dirt road and opened the door of the bus. An elderly woman collected her bundles and paper pokes and started down the aisle. As she reached the door, she turned, and, including every passenger in her backward look, said invitingly, "You folks better come home with me for dinner."

In that instant time turned backward straight to my childhood in Poor Fork. How long had it been since I had been treated to openhanded, openhearted, innate courtesy such as this old woman of the mountains was proffering? Not since I had left Poor Fork.

Like a tree in springtime when the sap begins to rise, I felt renewed and warmed and nourished, as if I had actually sat at the old woman's dinner table and partaken of her corn pone and beans. The courtesy and kindness and the helpful ways of people among whom I had lived for a few early years, and had taken for granted at the time, made me forget momentarily the ugly face that in my mind Harlan County now wore. Not everything good and lovely in these people had been destroyed, I contented myself. The certainty buoyed me up.

An hour later the bus driver pulled up in front of a drugstore and called out "Harlan!" I got off the bus and looked around me. The town was as quiet as if it were napping on a lazy summer afternoon. Only a few persons were on the streets. Three men sat on a bench in front of the drugstore, whittling and telling tales.

I went into the drugstore and inquired of the druggist if he knew Conway Smith, a cousin of mine. Yes, said he, he knew him well, and he would put me in touch with him on the telephone.

Shortly thereafter Conway arrived to take me to his house. Obviously the grapevine, originating in the drugstore, went to work, and that evening Conway's house was filled with people. Not only is blood relationship a strong tie in the mountains. Mountain origin itself admits into a close-knit circle all who are mountain born. Until late in the evening we sat talking. Among those present, one had gone to school to my father; another, the son of John Yearey, the other Democrat in our voting precinct at Poor Fork, recalled the rugged times our fathers had had on election days; another recalled our house as the meeting place for all who enjoyed singing to the accompaniment of my mother's little organ.

As we talked leisurely, their soft quiet mountain speech fell on my ears like a lullaby, and their flavorsome mountain words and phrases awoke in me memories of things I had not thought of in years. All about me were warmth and kindness. I began to wonder if the accounts I had read of Harlan County lawlessness could be true.

"What about all the trouble in the Harlan County mines a few years ago?" I asked.

"Oh, it was pretty rough around here for a while," someone said, "especially when all those meddlers from the outside came in here to push us around."

"And you didn't get involved?" I asked, remembering all the influential men who had turned down Dreiser's invitation to involve themselves.

"Oh, no, we weren't involved in any way," they assured me. "So long as nobody bothered us, we didn't bother anybody."

As I lay in bed in my cousin's house that night, I wondered who in the human race is an outsider, and when is a person concerned for human suffering a meddler; wondered if I would have had the courage to involve myself on behalf of free speech and free assembly in Harlan County in 1931; wondered if I would have helped to feed the miners in spite of threats; wondered if I had within me the spirit of reconciliation that the Quakers had within them.

But things were different now, I could see. World War II was in the making. Already the hot winds of coming holocaust were blowing across Europe. Soon would come the bang. Operators and miners were tooling up for the boom.

As I lay and wondered, I also made a discovery. The friends who had filled my cousin's house that evening had not come out of mere curiosity to see one who, starting life among them, had gone over the high rim of the mountains and out into the world. They had come out of affection and respect to see the daughter of George and Susan Caudill.

The following day, another cousin took me to Cumberland. In spite of the years that had passed, I foolishly looked for places and landmarks I had long ago known. But, as the ticket agent at Harrodsburg had warned me, Poor Fork was gone. It had indeed got itself a railroad, built beside the twisting Poor Fork River along which trains rumbled all day and all night—engines pulling gondolas full of coal from Lynch and Benham to Harlan and farther, and empty gondolas up to Benham and Lynch.

Going up in the world, I kept reminding myself, always necessitates change. But need the change be always for the worse? Poor Fork in changing to Cumberland had become

an ugly hit-or-miss town crammed into the narrow hollows backing off from the river, with houses sprawling up the mountainside. When my cousin pointed out to me a new development named the New York Addition, I recoiled. Why could not a town preserve its own personality, I wondered? Why need it ape alien places and people and customs?

We stopped first at the Sand Hill cemetery beside the river, where my cousin pointed out to me the grave of my twin sister, still marked by the field stones my father had placed there so long ago.

As we left the cemetery, I asked, "Where is the Dump? You know, where they rolled logs down the mountain into the river?"

"All the big trees were long ago cut off the mountains," my cousin told me. "Men came in and bought up the timber rights and skinned the mountains. The road cuts across the face of the Dump now. We'll drive by it soon."

We entered the town along the paved highway from Harlan and drove first to my old home, crossing the river by way of a bridge. I could accept the fact that the house went now by the sophisticated designation of 8 River Road and that children other than the Caudills were swinging on the front gate. And I had only admiration for the real estate developer who, when dividing my father's apple orchard into city lots and building a house on each lot, had had sufficient appreciation and sentiment to provide every householder with one apple tree in his yard.

It came as a shock, however, to discover Broomsedge Hill turned into a cemetery where graves were not marked with simple field stones, but with stones of granite on which names and sentimental epitaphs were engraved. At least, I comforted myself, Jim and Cassie Huff rested there, near the place where Clara and I had labored so hard and with so little recompense on Will's playhouse.

I felt a sinister change had come over that part of Appalachia that was mine. The river seemed the most changed, and all for the worse. I remembered it as clear and clean and deep, and sparkling in the sun. I suddenly recalled a particular summer afternoon when my father took me fishing for the first time. We seated ourselves comfortably on the giant roots of an ancient sycamore growing beside the river, and I was instructed by my father that I must not talk aloud else the fish would be scared away. He first baited my hook and put the rod in my hand. Then he baited his own, and dropped it into a deep pothole. There we sat companionably with the sun going down at our backs and casting long shadows across the water, my father speaking to me now and then in a low, quiet voice, I answering in whispers. He caught the fish, a "passel" of them, we would have said, strung them on a twig, and put them back into the water until we were ready to go home. I did not recall that I caught any fish. But I remembered the thrill that went through me every time I had a nibble. It was as if I had received a message from some kindly inhabitant of a deep, dark, underwater world. Perhaps catching a fish might have been more exciting. I, however, was quiveringly satisfied with nibbles.

Now there were no fish in the river. There were no deep potholes where fish could live. I had not been mistaken as I rode along in the bus, thinking that the rivers were shallower than I remembered them. The Poor Fork now was not only low; it was apparently the local refuse dump. Tin cans, pop bottles, and discarded automobile tires lined the banks, while the river itself was full of debris which apparently it was too sluggish to move along.

Across the river, on the mountainside, both above and below the road, clung unbelievably unsightly shacks. Dirty-faced, ragged children played on coal piles in dirty dooryards. Open privies drained into the river. Here was poverty of the most shameful sort.

"Nobody ever lived like that!" I heard myself saying in despair. "Nobody was rich. But certainly nobody was poor. Not like that."

"Oh," said my cousin, "there are plenty of rich people about. They own the mines or manage them. Those people you see up there are miners. They've come in here from every holler in Appalachia and every country in the world, I reckon."

Late that afternoon I took a bus for home, refreshed by the renewal with my childhood, chilled by the ugliness and devastation I had witnessed in a part of the world that had been intimately mine, and with my mind filled with a torment created by one question: Who is my brother's keeper?

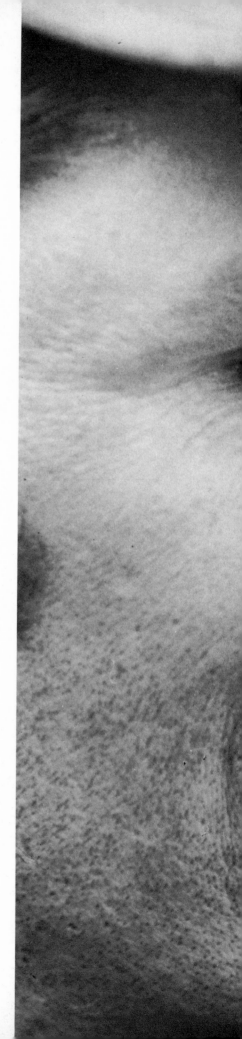

3 Today

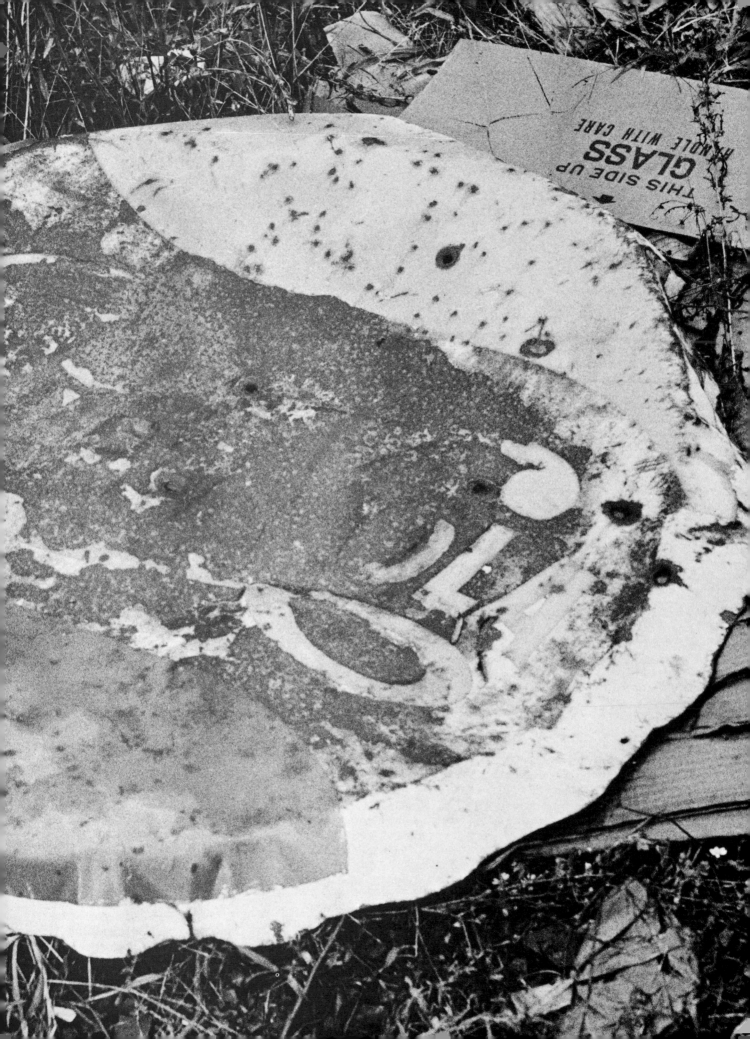

The question that nagged me as I rode away from Cumberland on the bus in the summer of 1938 is, of course, as old as Cain. It stayed with me, though I lived many miles from Southern Appalachia and for several years was in no position to do anything about it.

Finally, in the autumn of 1953, my husband, James Ayars, and I stopped in Cumberland on the return trip from an extended vacation in the South. With the exception of a few of my cousins, we found no one I had known from my childhood.

I did not know how the mountain people would react to my Michigan-reared husband nor he to them. Ayars is a name foreign to Southern Appalachia. Caudill is as common in eastern Kentucky as Anderson in Minnesota. In the thin telephone directory of a Kentucky mountain town of 1,774 population, James found listed 69 Caudills, 16 Smiths, 7 Joneses, and 6 Johnsons.

James discovered a getting-acquainted formula that worked like magic. He told everyone he met that he had married a Caudill from Harlan County, and immediately he was received into the inner circle of mountaineers as if he too had been born among them.

Soon we became like homing pigeons, returning to the Kentucky mountains two or more times each year—six times in one year.

We went in the fall partly because of the panorama of brilliant colors spread like a Persian carpet on the slopes of the mountains. We went in the spring partly because the first prolonged onrush of warm days brought out the white delicate blossoms of the service berry (as children we had given the name of this tree its old English pronunciation and had spelled it as we pronounced it—sarvis berry), the white splashes of the dogwood, the magenta stain of the Judas tree among the gray trunks of mountain forests, and, in the clearings, just as I had remembered them from my childhood, spring beauties and blue-eyed grass running down the mountains to meet us.

In whichever season, we went mainly to be with friends—a steadily enlarging circle of friends, some of them natives, some of them transplanted outlanders who had found in the mountains quiet and beauty, and a generous and responsive people to work among. In the natives we knew best, we found

the traits I had remembered from my childhood in Poor Fork, traits that appealed to James as much as to me: the unhurrried pace, the earthy wisdom, the good common sense, the subtle wit, the independence, and the unobtrusive innate courtesy.

But along any mountain road we traveled, we found disquieting signs—weatherbeaten shacks with large numbers of poorly clothed, dirty children playing in littered dooryards; neglected, dilapidated schoolhouses; tiny, square-steepled churches from whose pulpits preachers faced empty benches and a few old ladies and shouted sermons about a life of idyllic ease in a beautiful alabaster city in the sky—a hereafter life to compensate for the hardships and sorrows of the earthly vale of tears.

From our friends we heard stories of mountain men who had been totally disabled in mine accidents and who were finding their Workmen's Compensation allotments pitifully insufficient to feed and clothe their large families; stories of families that, after two or three generations on relief, were living aimless, hopeless lives of perpetual degrading poverty. We heard stories of able-bodied but unskilled men who could find no jobs and who, in order that their families might have food from relief agencies, had picked up and gone away, where no one knew. We heard stories of girls leaving home to marry at fifteen or sixteen and shortly thereafter coming home pregnant and bringing their jobless husbands with them. In some shacks, we learned, the mother of a large family that included husband, married sons and daughters, their spouses, and their children, was the sole wage earner.

Happier stories we heard, too. One concerned the father of thirteen children. Disabled by a lung disease contracted in the mines, he had gone with his small income from Workmen's Compensation back to his rocky hillside farm up Little Laurel Creek, where he and his wife were raising their children with joyous affection, instilling in them a sense of individual worth and independence, and maintaining the family solidarity I had known among the people of Poor Fork.

In contrast to the poverty and want we saw along the roads we traveled was the enormous mineral wealth of the region. Since 1944, the output of

Southern Appalachian coal had exceeded 200 million tons annually. Valued at approximately five dollars per ton, it brought to stockholders in coal companies in excess of one billion dollars a year. Geologists have estimated that, at the 1944 rate of output, the mountains of eastern Kentucky and eastern Tennessee contain coal deposits sufficient to last one thousand years.

During the period of our visits to Southern Appalachia, we watched one notable change come over the mountains. We did not see the beginning of it. That took place in the late 1940's when a bulldozer dug out a roadway along the side of a mountain, uprooting trees in its path and sending showers of boulders down the mountain, along with loosened earth, to choke the stream below.

Arriving near the top of the mountain, the bulldozer stripped the soil from a seam of coal. A giant mechanized shovel lifted the coal out of the earth and dumped it into trucks that had toiled up the mountain along the road dug out by the bulldozer. Truck followed truck in steady procession until the shovel had gouged out of the mountain all the coal it could get at. This operation was called strip mining.

The first such operation in Harlan County was, seemingly, an insignificant one, though it left mountaineers wondering about the wanton destruction of the surface soil and trees, the choking of the stream, and the ugly gash left on the side of the mountain.

The operation had been carried out under the privileges granted the party of the second part by a mountaineer and his wife who, long since dead, had signed their names at the end of a long-form deed. That strip mining, bulldozers, giant mechanized shovels, and all the appurtenances and refinements of strip mining were unheard of when the deeds were signed was a matter lightly dismissed by the party of the second part.

Mountaineers who observed the operation, learning that it had been carried out under the provisions of a long-form deed, looked up the deeds to their own property. Most of them, the heirs of earlier mountaineers, finding they held deeds of the same sort, shrugged their shoulders and hoped this new method of taking coal from the earth would go away.

Strip mining did not by any means go away, but as late as 1957 only 5 percent of eastern Kentucky's annual coal output was strip mined. After 1957, strip mines, which could produce coal at a much lower cost than deep pit mines, even those equipped with modern automatic machinery, multiplied like rabbits.

Here and there a cry of anger went up from some mountaineer whose farm was being bulldozed down the mountain into his front yard—a poor farm by most standards, but one that had given the mountaineer and his family a subsistence living, had helped him and his wife to feed and clothe their children and to keep them in school. But the paternalism of the coal companies had robbed the mountaineer of much of his independence and initiative. He had no one now, except the same coal companies, to tell him what to do, and they told him to forget it, since there was nothing he could do about it.

When the mountaineer consulted a lawyer, he was told that, under the terms of the long-form deed, his grandparents had signed away any possible right he might have had to stop the bulldozer. So, mad but helpless, he sat down in his splint-bottomed chair, tilted it back against the porch wall, and cursed as he watched the bulldozer scrape away the soil on which he had raised his corn, his sorghum, his potatoes, and his fall beans, break over the trees in his patch of timber, and push soil and trees together down the slope, burying the pasture on which he had grazed his cow. But however loud his cry and however vehement his curses, they were drowned out by the roar of more and ever bigger and more powerful bulldozers and mechanized shovels at work on dozens of mountains.

A few mountaineers whose land was being despoiled by strip mining took their cases against the coal companies into court. But in every case the judge, basing his decision on an antiquated long-form deed, ruled in favor of the coal company.

One fall when we went back to Harlan County, I found the mountains that I had always thought of as in some way belonging to me—Pine and Big Black—had been despoiled and desecrated by man's unbelievable cupidity and folly. Big Black, with a long, ugly gash near its summit, looked like a monarch with

a noose around his neck.

Not only have many miners lost their farms through strip mining; an even greater number of them have lost their jobs through mechanization that includes strip mining and a more recent development, augering.

Augering is a method of coal mining employed where a bulldozer can clear on a mountainside a bench or shelf wide enough for operation of the necessary machinery. A huge steel auger, mechanically driven, with a diameter equivalent to the thickness of the seam of coal—sixteen to thirty inches or more—bores horizontally into the seam for perhaps two hundred feet. The coal flows from the auger onto a conveyor that carries it to one of many trucks lined up and waiting to go. One auger may average more than twenty-six tons of coal per man-shift. Although somewhat less destructive of the surface than strip mining, augering leaves its ugly scars on mountain slopes and contaminates streams and wells below.

Except for truck drivers, most of the men employed in strip mining and augering must be highly skilled in the use of complicated machinery; many of them have been imported with the machinery. These methods of mining therefore provide few jobs for the men of the mountains, and the employment rate among mountaineers is correspondingly downward as mining approaches complete mechanization.

The devastation wrought by strip mining and augering is as obvious in the people as in the mountains themselves. The mountaineer who in previous years made a living at mining and, as a member of the United Mine Workers, received for himself and his family a few notable fringe benefits, such as free hospital service in any of the eight finely equipped and well-staffed UMW hospitals in the Southern Appalachian mining area, has had to accept one of two choices. Hundreds of mountaineers, skilled only as miners, have chosen to leave the mountains to look uncertainly for jobs elsewhere. Others, notably the partially disabled, have chosen to stay in the mountains and go on relief. Staying or leaving, the mountaineer plods along in his slow gait with the sour taste of hopelessness in his mouth.

Dark though the total situation is in Southern Appalachia, the area has its

bright spots. Over many years, it has felt the enlightening influence of small centers of culture, most of them established by outlanders in the early part of the present century. Many of these centers were financed by church denominations, a few by individuals, and some by nonsectarian groups that depended upon voluntary contributions.

The people of Southern Appalachia have long aroused the sympathies of compassionate outlanders. One such outlander, J. C. Campbell, worked among the mountaineers for many years, wrote about them in a definitive book called *The Southern Highlander and His Homeland,* and established the Council of the Southern Mountains, the most important agency working for the welfare and enrichment of the mountain people on an area-wide basis. Another outlander, Perley F. Ayer, a native of Maine, is now the vigorous and challenging executive director of the Council.

Most of the centers of culture were settlement schools, or boarding schools, for boys and girls of high school age. And most of them were in isolated rural areas. Some of the students lived near the schools, but most of them lived far from any school, at the heads of inaccessible hollows or along rushing creeks that were impassable in winter.

Wherever such a settlement school or other center of culture was established there was an oasis of sobriety and stability in a society that had accepted periodic drunkenness and violence as normal ways of behavior. The Presbyterian School at Buckhorn, Redbird Mission at Beverly, the Pine Mountain Settlement School at Pine Mountain, the Hindman Settlement School at Hindman, Homeplace at Ary, and Caney Creek Junior College (now Alice Lloyd College) at Pippa Passes were a few of the many such centers in Kentucky.

Although the character of the settlement schools that still exist has changed in the past fifty years, and some of their programs have been taken over by county school systems, they continue to be centers of culture where the effects of isolation are broken down and children and adults are encouraged to respect and keep alive the desirable skills and folkways of their ancestors. Here children are introduced to the world outside the

JOIN MISSION SAFETY-

"The toll of injuries and the cost of accidents must be reduced again and again."

Lyndon B. Johnson

WORK SAFELY- "REDUCE FEDERAL
EMPLOYEE WORK INJURIES 30% BY 1970"

FEDERAL SAFETY COUNCIL

mountains and are prepared as thoroughly as possible to fulfill their lives in or out of the mountains.

A recent cultural development in Southern Appalachia is the establishment of county libraries and bookmobiles. In eastern Kentucky, many county libraries have been established with the aid of federal funds allocated by the State Department of Libraries. A prerequisite to the establishment of a public library in any Kentucky county is a self-imposed library tax voted by the people. Ten years ago, a public library in a Kentucky mountain county was as scarce as a robin in January. Now many counties have not only a main library in the county seat but a branch library in another part of the county, and perhaps even a bookmobile or two.

Neither libraries nor schools nor the Council of the Southern Mountains can cope with the evils of strip mining, of laws that allow a nonrenewable natural resource to be hauled out without a penny of tax revenue, of an economy based on a resource concerning which the people have had no voice.

In 1965, the Congress of the United States passed the Appalachian Regional Development Act, which had been proposed by President Kennedy and strongly supported by President Johnson. For its implementation, Congress appropriated the sum of $1,092,400,000, and President Johnson signed the bill on March 9.

The Act is the direct result of the combined efforts of the Conference of Appalachian Governors and the President's Appalachian Regional Commission. In making its legislative recommendations, the President's Commission called attention to the fact that Appalachia is "plagued by low income, high unemployment, lack of urbanization, low educational achievement, and relatively low living standards."

To "restore the region's economic vitality," the Commission proposed action on several fronts. Accordingly, in making its appropriation, Congress designated that, of the total amount, 840 million dollars should be spent on building roads; 41 million dollars on the construction of comprehensive health centers to serve multicounty areas; 36.5 million dollars to fill in underground mines, remove refuse piles, permit the reclamation of

strip-mined public land, and establish a study to recommend long-range programs for strip mine reclamation; 90 million dollars to be spent toward the construction of airports, colleges, junior colleges, and hospitals; and lesser amounts for water resource surveys, sewage treatment facilities, vocational education construction, land stabilization and erosion control, timber development, and administration.

Between Act and accomplishment lie many a pitfall and many a long, dreary mile. Wherever James and I went in Southern Appalachia, we asked people —waitresses, students, teachers, school administrators, public officials, farmers, housewives—their opinions of the Act. Some had never heard of it. Some thought the federal government was up to its old tricks of doling out charity and so perpetuating the dependency of mountaineers already on relief. Some thought the Act had the cart before the horse by appropriating so little for education and so much for roads. At least one school administrator thought that it confounded confusion and in no place so manifestly as in Washington. Still others thought that, when the Act expires in 1971, the local politician will be richer and the poor mountaineers will still be on relief, just as they were when the Act went into effect. And there were those who thought it best to wait and see.

Back at home, James and I decided we wanted to talk to still more people in Southern Appalachia, both mountaineers and outlanders who had lived in the mountains and worked with the mountain people over a long period of years. We wanted to know not only their opinions of the Appalachian Regional Development Act, but their reactions to economic problems, especially those related to strip mining, and their estimate of the quality of life in the mountains.

In search of answers to our questions, James and I and photographer Edward Wallowitch of New York made two trips through Southern Appalachia, the first in a recent July, the second in the following October. We started our first trip at Asheville and traveled through the timbered Blue Ridge mountains of North Carolina and the mining areas of eastern Tennessee and eastern Kentucky. We began the second at Pineville, drove along blacktopped highways and dusty back roads,

zigzagging through eastern Kentucky, southwestern Virginia, and western West Virginia.

James carried a tape recorder, Edward three cameras and a bag full of film, and I a notebook in which were listed the times and places of appointments for interviews with people in the area. We soon learned we needed no appointments. Everyone we interviewed talked freely and urged us to talk with others living at the head of the next hollow or on the other side of the mountain, so anxious were all to convince us of the common hatred of strip mining and to air their opinions of federal aid.

Our first interview was with Dr. W. D. Weatherford, who lives at the end of a narrow, winding road halfway up a mountain in North Carolina. Dr. Weatherford has spent most of his ninety years working with and for mountaineers. This one-time educator, Methodist preacher, Y.M.C.A. official, and vice-president of Berea College sees three principal problems in the Southern Appalachians.

"The problem that gives us the most trouble, because a lot of other things depend on it, is the economic problem," Dr. Weatherford told Edward, James, and me as we sat in the book-lined study of the home he calls "Far Horizons." "If you don't have money, you can't have schools, you can't have churches, you can't even have decent homes. I don't think it's the most important problem, but it's basic.

"The state governments have just sat by and let the big boys come in and take everything that is worth anything. In Kentucky, it's been the coal; in North Carolina, it's been the timber; in Georgia, it's been a combination of various things. The state and local governments have just sat down and done nothing. They could have said to the people who were strip mining, 'You can't strip mine and pile the soil over on the side of the mountain so that when the rains come it washes down over the farms below. Furthermore, you can't take coal out of this state without compensating in taxes.'

"The big boys came into Kentucky and took the coal out and left the state without providing any just compensation. Kentucky, West Virginia, eastern Tennessee, and parts of Alabama are coal mining sections.

We've got no coal in North Carolina. Our chief resource was timber. We had the finest timber the world ever saw. When I first came into these mountains sixty years ago, it was not uncommon to see plenty of trees that were four feet at the butt and rising a hundred feet high. Perfectly beautiful! The big boys who had the money came in here and went to the little farmers, as they did in Kentucky, and said, 'Now, we don't want your land; we just want your trees.' And they bought the right to lumber the land for nothing almost, and literally stripped the mountains. Mount Mitchell was covered with balsam, and they built a railroad up there and took millions of feet of balsam lumber out of the region.

"While they were doing it, they were controlling the local politicians, because the local politicians didn't have sense enough to control themselves. They were keeping taxes low and putting the money they saved in their pockets.

"Our second problem is ignorance. The average educational level in our region is 7.2 years. Sixty-three percent of the boys leave school without getting through the eighth grade. They become dropouts. They go hunting for a job. In most cases they can't get one because they haven't had enough education to take the training needed to work in it. I figure we've got nearly a million people who are below the level of getting a job that requires any skill.

"Our third problem in the mountains is a big one, one of the very big ones. We've got no sense of community responsibility. The little one-room district school used to be a grass-roots institution that got out to the people and helped to develop a sense of community responsibility. But that's gone now. The one grass-roots institution we've got left is the country church. But the country preacher with his little bit of a congregation doesn't build community spirit. He says to his people, 'Now you stick to this church.' That is, let the rest of the community go to the dogs.''

Preachers assigned to mountain churches, Dr. Weatherford emphasized, should be intelligent, broadly trained, interested more in community welfare than in denominationalism, and willing to devote their lives to the mountaineers. Emphasis on denominationalism has robbed the mountains of community leadership,

64

he maintained. He complained that in the past the churches have assigned their most ignorant preachers to the mountains and have moved to the cities any who showed promise of development.

"Mountaineers don't organize much," he said. "The little mountain farms never called for organization. There was one man on a farm and he ran everything on the place. I was born on a farm like that, and there was no organization there because there was nobody to organize. My daddy and I did the work. My daddy said, 'Take the hoe and let's go to work.' That was all the organization there was. But people can be trained to organize. This poverty business is a long, hard pull. If we can get enough people to work at it, we'll come through all right. There's got to be hope for Southern Appalachia. You can't throw away seven million people, you know. You've got to do something with them.''

The mountaineer, Dr. Weatherford told us, in thinking about his problems doesn't see that he is partly responsible for the community. "One of our big problems is that we're still bossed by capital, not people. And I'm against that.''

Dr. Weatherford is of the opinion that the Appalachian Regional Development Act will "help a lot." But he does not believe it will give everybody a job.

"We don't have enough jobs to give everybody a job, as we define a job now, and as far as I can see we never will. There's only one way out, and that is to reevaluate what we mean by a job and include a much larger class of services in it. We should say to a person, 'If you really serve, you've got a job. If you're doing something for people, that's a job.' There are lots of services that people don't now think of as jobs. Visiting the sick is an example, doing some nursing service—all sorts of things that people have done voluntarily and without pay. These are just as much jobs as making carpets.''

A student of the history of Southern Appalachia, Dr. Weatherford believes that people of the mountains have lost much of their independence—once a characteristic trait.

"That's because they've had to be dependent," he told us. "They've had to take charity. They've had to do all sorts of things that eat away character. And sending old clothes and shoes down here is not the answer, either.

That makes me so mad I want to fight. We've got much bigger things to do than that. We've got to help lift these people out of their ignorance, and out of their poverty, and out of their deterministic theories, their fundamentalist theories, and free them. But I believe they've got the stuff in them and we can do it. The people of these mountains, after all, have done a great deal for America. They've given us a sense of independence we wouldn't have had without them. The first three declarations of independence in this country were written in these mountains long before Thomas Jefferson wrote his Declaration of Independence. The first was written in Wautauga, Tennessee, the second in Fincastle County, Virginia, and the third in Mecklenburg County, at Charlotte, North Carolina.''

In 1930, lumberman E. O. Robinson, who had realized a fortune from the timber rights he had bought up in eastern Kentucky and who wanted to leave some of his wealth to serve the people living in the area where he had made it, established the E. O. Robinson Mountain Fund. Robinson had some definite ideas about how he did not want the money from the fund spent. He did not want to found a boarding school, for he believed children should live in their own homes, and each community should have its own school. He wanted his money invested in some project that would benefit an entire community in special ways the community itself could not afford.

To carry out his ideas, Homeplace at Ary, on Troublesome Creek, was founded. Robinson asked Miss Lula M. Hale, a young mountain woman educated at Eastern Kentucky State Teachers College, to become the first director of Homeplace.

We talked with Miss Hale one morning in the big living room of the log house on the well-kept grounds of Homeplace.

Miss Hale's early life is typical of that of many mountaineers who put an education first in their lives. Born in Letcher County, Miss Hale moved with her family to live near Hindman in Knott County, where her father obtained a job operating the light plant for the Hindman Settlement School. Miss Hale attended the Settlement School until she received her diploma. From there she went to college. After receiving her degree, she taught school and helped a younger brother and sister through college.

START
THE DAY
WITH GOD
Caney Mennonite Church
1 Mi.
STOP
DO
NOT
PASS

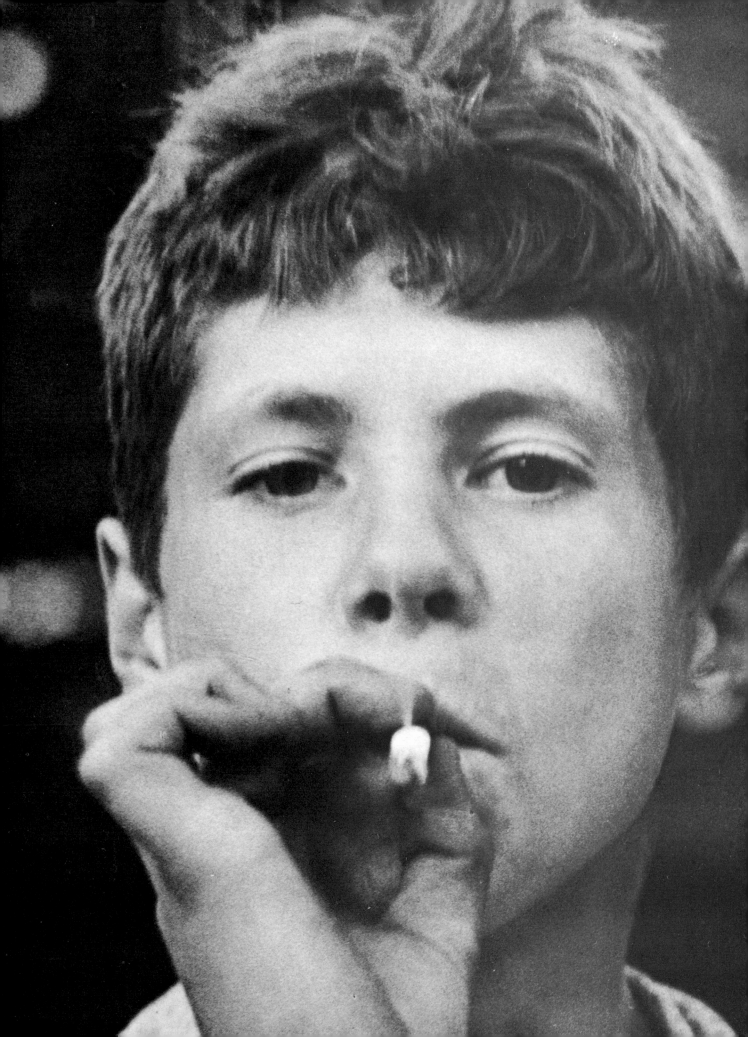

"I felt responsible for them," she said to us. "Most of the Hales felt they wanted an education."

For nearly forty years, Homeplace, under Miss Hale's direction, has served not only the Perry County community of which it is a part, but also a much wider area, through bookmobiles, through home economics taught at the institution and in the homes, through recreation for young people, through introduction of improved methods of growing field crops and livestock, and through health programs administered first by clinics, today by a well-staffed hospital.

Although few people of the older generations living along Troublesome Creek within the Homeplace area have received more than an eighth grade education, a large number of their children have attended college and many of them have returned to teach in the area.

In spite of this unusual record for an Appalachian community, the Homeplace area has its quota of dropouts, particularly among the boys of 14, 15, and 16 who consider education too long and too slow a process for earning enough money to make a down payment on a third- or fourth-hand automobile.

Pat Edwards, formerly of Speedwell in the mountains of eastern Tennessee, lives and works now in Dayton, Ohio. Her story of education and family solidarity is not unlike that of Miss Hale.

We met Pat while she was attending a conference, sponsored by the Council of the Southern Mountains, on the problems of mountaineers who migrate to northern cities.

"I have eight younger brothers and sisters," Pat told us. "I have a brother in the Air Force and a sister who will be a junior at Lincoln Memorial College this fall. I felt that if I could get a job in the city I could help my family —we don't have very much—with clothing, food, or whatever they need. I felt too that I could help my younger sisters go to college, and perhaps go on to college myself, which I am doing. I attend Sinclair College at night and work during the day."

We asked Pat her opinion of the Appalachian Regional Development Act.

"I know we haven't had the opportunities to move ahead as fast as the rest of the nation," said Pat. "And all at once the rest of the nation is going to come in and bring us up to the twentieth century. But we have some qualities I hope they don't take away from us. We are individuals. And we have close family ties. In my family, for instance, we had a couple of debts come up which my father couldn't pay. I thought, here's this money I was saving for my education, but my family comes first. And really I don't have any feelings because I have to pay. You know, I had to pay those debts off for my family because this is something you do. It is part of your family. You help them regardless of the situation or whatever problems they have."

Pat's experience away from the mountains is typical of the experiences of thousands of mountaineers who go to the city, find a job, and quietly make their way upward. Offering as her skills a high school education, a knowledge of shorthand, and two years of typing in high school, Pat found a job as clerk-typist, typing insurance forms in the business office of a Dayton hospital.

"We're given ratings after we've worked in the office six months," Pat told us, "and my boss was very pleased with my work and my general attitude. Quite a number of people work in this office, and my boss told another girl, when he told her her rating, 'I wish I had more like you and Miss Edwards because you work and don't talk all the time.' Recently another job opened up, which, if I could get it, would mean quite a promotion for me. My boss recommended me for the transfer, and the job was given me, even though I had had no experience with a soundscriber and had to learn it on the job."

At Buckhorn, Kentucky, we talked with Mary Wright, a social worker for the Presbyterian Child Welfare Agency. Miss Wright, a New Englander, made her first contribution to the mountain people by serving as a courier—in other words, by taking care of horses and going on errands—for nurses of the Frontier Nursing Service. Believing she had found the people among whom she wished to spend her life, she returned East to study social work and eventually took up residence on the campus of the Presbyterian School at Buckhorn, to work with the children there.

We asked Miss Wright about school dropouts.

"The first thing that causes children to drop out of school," Miss Wright said, "is their parents' attitude toward school. Some of the parents have had very little, if any, schooling. They think it is a good idea, but they don't really understand what it is, and, if something else comes up that seems important, this tends to get priority. Therefore the children don't start off with the feeling that school is very important. Therefore they don't get to school regularly, therefore they miss out on some of the work—they get behind, they don't succeed—therefore they get to feeling defeated, therefore they lose interest. And therefore they miss more school. It's a vicious circle."

Mary Wright agrees with many others in saying that politics controls a large part of the life of any mountain community, that politics controls many school appointments, and that this situation "doesn't necessarily mean good education."

"You have seen a great many people who have to depend on welfare," we said. "What does being on welfare do to them?"

"People here have become more and more dependent on welfare," Miss Wright told us, "because they do not have the opportunities to become independent of it. I do not go along with the critics who blame these people for becoming dependent on welfare. Any of us would become dependent if we were in their situation. This is the only vision they have of a secure life, of stable income, of something they can count on from one month to the next. And they're going to hang on to that unless and until society gives them something equally secure to take hold of. At the point where society gives them something equally secure, they're going to take hold of it, and then we won't have them on welfare.

"You'd be surprised at the number of retarded people who will never be able to absorb the kind of training they need for the modern world. Let's accept this fact: these people are not going to be able to make it. Let's give them a decent living and hope that their children will rise above them. And let's not condemn them and walk over them and push them down and make them feel bad and pass a feeling of bitterness on to their children.

"Let government assume its role and support these people who might have been able to get along in years gone by but who are not able to now."

"I'm getting the feeling," Edward commented, "there's got to be a change of attitude in the people themselves—a change from the 'Poor-me!-I-know-I'm-a-worthless-soul' attitude. It's hidden in the children, but it seems to come out later in life when people are given to a more overt expression of the attitude."

"You certainly find this attitude in many people," Miss Wright answered. "But you also find many who have a lot of self-respect and who resent the rest of the world seeming to say 'Poor Appalachia!' They say, 'There's nothing poor about us. We can solve our own problems, and you can get out of here. We're doing all right.' You get some pretty strong feelings on that side."

One of the programs we heard most about in the mountains was the work experience program set up by the Office of Economic Opportunity for Unemployed Fathers.

"The Unemployed Fathers program has been a great boon, really," said Miss Wright. "Of course, there are weaknesses, but, when you compare what the men in this program are doing with what they were doing, you see progress. The men view their jobs as work; they are employed. But the idea of the program is that this work is temporary until they find other employment. My experience is that most of them are not actively looking for other employment. What they would find would be irregular, seasonal work, without security. Along with this program we should be making efforts to get other jobs available so that, when the program stops, these men will have something to do."

The kind of work set aside for the Unemployed Fathers in the Work Experience Program varies from area to area and depends on the direction of the local committee in charge. The morale of the workers depends to a great extent on their supervisor.

Brit Wilder, in charge of maintenance at Pine Mountain Settlement School, is also supervisor of a group of Unemployed Fathers who work mainly on the campus of the school. The afternoon we observed the men at work, they were building a footbridge across Isaac's Run and were very proud of a couple of stringers they had used to give the bridge a natural arch.
70

Wilder told us about one man in his group of Unemployed Fathers. "One of our Unemployed Fathers should have been on total disabled," he said. "He had a terrible back, and he's had an operation. He was to the point where he had give up. Well, we got him here, and I said to him, 'I think we can find somethin' for you to do.' Well, he couldn't do anything. He had this back he was afraid of.

"It was a disc he'd had removed. He was in the coal mines, and he got the best of care at the miners' hospital. But then he couldn't work in the mines any longer, and he had been on welfare for some time and then they said they was not goin' to have him on that any more 'cause he could get on the job as fathers. So he had to take it. Then he had to find some place that would take him, because this is supposed to be a work program. He had to work. And he's learned to bottom a chair. You should see the things that that man has done, and he's a livin' again. So we feel like that we have given him a life instead of sayin', 'Well, we just can't use a man that can't work.' Why, we've got chairs all over that he's made. He done that for awhile and then he started out one day with the other men. The only thing I said was, 'Now, be careful of your back, Clem,' when he was goin' out to lift or somethin'. But he goes out and works with us in a good spirit, and he's a livin' as far as he's concerned.

"He goes to school, too. They all have to go to school. But they've worked so long, and they're so used to doin' things with their hands, it's so strange for them to figure out that it's some educational system they've got to have to make a livin'."

In contrast is the story of an Unemployed Father whose personal experience is reported by Larry Greathouse, field representative of the Council of Southern Mountains, writing in *Mountain Life & Work*. " 'The most skill training I have had on this project,' said the Unemployed Father, 'is how to use a pick and shovel. I did that when I was 10 years old. And because I didn't vote the right way last election I was moved to a work project at the other end of the county. I have to hitch-hike 40 miles to work each morning, hitch-hike back home in the early afternoon, hitch-hike back to the school for classes in the evening and get back home about 9:00 o'clock each night. Right now our supervisor doesn't

allow us a lunch break. When we do get a smoke break, we are asked to go into the woods and keep out of sight. We are treated like convicts. We might as well have balls and chains on our ankles. I have been to the public assistance office and the employment service office five times and not yet have I had a hearing on these complaints.' "*

We spoke to Mrs. Billie Jean Cawood, supervisor of elementary education in Harlan County, about the high dropout rate among high school students in the mountains.

"In many instances," she said, "the lack of interest in attending school begins in the first grade. Many children would drop out in the third grade if they weren't required to be in school until they reach the age of sixteen. This is partly due to apathy in the home. We've been working with the parents to try to help them realize the value of an education. We already see some improvement.

"We are hoping that the classes established for the Unemployed Fathers will be a factor in helping parents realize the need for an education. Just last week a Negro father on the Unemployed Fathers program showed me a new dictionary he had bought. He told me what he had paid for it. It was not an expensive dictionary but it was a good one and he was quite proud of it. Now the children of that father, I feel, will want to learn when they get to school because their father will encourage them to learn."

For two years, Mrs. Cawood and her husband taught school in Florida. They returned to their native Kentucky partly because they missed the mountains and partly because they found the mountain children possessed of greater emotional stability than those they taught in Florida.

Effects of the low salary schedule that, at the time, placed Kentucky forty-sixth in the nation, were being felt in Harlan County as in other parts of the mountains. In the spring, the county superintendent of schools had hired twenty more certified teachers than he would have teaching positions in the fall, knowing that, by the beginning of school, many of his teachers would have gone to states where higher salaries were paid. We learned later

*Greathouse, Larry, "The Weaknesses Are Appearing," *Mountain Life & Work,* Vol. 40, No. 3, Fall, 1965.

that, for the same reason, the superintendent of schools in adjoining Letcher County commonly hired thirty to forty more certified teachers than he had teaching positions. Even though supposedly extra numbers of certified teachers had been hired, both counties usually began the fall terms with several emergency teachers, teachers whose training was below the state standards.

When Jerry Workman left the Pine Mountain Settlement School to teach a class of gifted children in a privileged community, he thought that he was through with teaching mountain children. But the next year he was back at Pine Mountain. Why?

"Probably the mountains themselves had something to do with my coming back, because I have always loved the mountains. I like the woods. I was reared in the country.

"The people here are very friendly when you go to their homes. They treat you very well and make you feel that you are welcome. In most of the homes, I feel that if I want to go to the kitchen and get a cup of coffee I am free to do so.

"The children here are more interesting to teach than the ones I taught last year. They have not been exposed to so many things and they are easy to motivate. They are very willing to try to learn. There seems to be within me a feeling that I am accomplishing more here than where I was teaching last year. There seems to be more that I can give to the children here."

Among the old people with whom we talked, we did not find any who had not coveted a good education for their children. Although they themselves lacked formal education and made their living with their hands, they had tremendous respect for book learning. One such person was eighty-year-old Mrs. Jalia Turner Sebastian, who lives near Booneville, Kentucky. A few miles from her house we had stopped to watch a group of Unemployed Fathers building a bridge over a small stream. The supervisor, Roscoe Sebastian, told us he had attended Berea College one year but did not return because his father was ill with asthma and he felt he should stay at home to work on the farm. His own son was now attending college. He urged us to go to see his parents.

Roscoe's mother welcomed us warmly and invited us into the living room where her husband, breathing hoarsely, sat hunched sidewise in an upholstered chair. We told Mrs. Sebastian we had talked with her son.

"You mean Roscoe? Well, I got two children," she said. "You want me to tell you about the other one? He lives in Ohio. He went to college. We wanted Roscoe to go on to college too but he wanted to stop. I'd a graduated him if he'd went on. I says, 'You'll make a better livin' and an easier one if you'll go on.'"

About her son in Ohio, Mrs. Sebastian told us, "He works for the government. He's been a workin' for the government and has been overseas for the government seven times. He's a wonderful worker. I don't guess he could ever be beat. He went through college and he and his wife are both college graduates. Roscoe, now, he liked the farm work and like that. Now he works. But hit's farm work."

"But don't you think both kinds of work are important, Mrs. Sebastian?" I asked. "Both kinds are needed?"

"But the other one," she said proudly, "he works with a pencil."

Mrs. Rosa Belle Kirk Evans, eighty-six and widowed, owns and operates a small country store on Pucketts Creek near St. Charles, Virginia. Born and reared not far from the site of the store, Mrs. Evans, alert and staunchly independent, together with her husband raised and educated five sons and two daughters.

St. Charles was once a mining area, with several large companies operating nearby during the boom days of World War I and immediately afterward. Now the coal mining industry there has dwindled to a few truck mines.

We talked with Mrs. Evans in her store as a few customers, neighbors of hers, came, waited on themselves, and went.

"None of my children didn't never work in the mines," Mrs. Evans told us. "They wasn't no better than nobody else, but I tried to get 'em in shape till they could work other places. I dreaded the mines. My husband didn't ever work in the mines. He worked on the farm. We had just a little farm. Hit was a mountain farm but hit produced good if hit was worked. We always had plenty to live on."

Mrs. Evans painted in colorful words the ways of mountain people of an earlier day—the hard work that went into farming; the making of garments out of cloth woven of wool sheared from their own sheep; the cooking of simple nourishing meals on a stepstove; the good times country folks had at log rollings, clearings, and quiltings.

"But now," she said, "they have what they call the welfare here, and they's a lot of people livin' on that. Hit makes sorry people. Lazy. A lot of 'em jest get on hit to keep from workin'. I think this makes sorry people. We was always taught to work. My father always raised us up that way, and I raised my children to work.

"My mother, now, was old," she continued, "and she was with me at the last. They wanted her to go on relief. She'd had a stroke and she wasn't able to work. But she didn't go on relief. She said her husband, my father, had left her enough to live on."

Mrs. Evans, from her long observation in one area, feels that mountain people have changed. Folks had such a good time doing things together, she said, speaking of the old days. "And they wasn't—I don't know what you call it now. Seems like they's selfish—ever'body's for theirselves and don't care for nobody else. Mostly ever'body's kindly selfish any more. And they don't help each other, like they used to. I know they don't. I've lived a long time and I've learned a right smart of things."

Mrs. Evans told us that her parents had no formal education and she had very little. But she was proud that all her children had much greater educational opportunities than had been available to her. One son, she seemed to think, had overdone education.

"Your son Wilson got his doctorate at Teachers College in New York," we reminded her.

"Yes," Mrs. Evans said, "he went and got it. Hain't been long since he went and took a little more of somethin' at the University at Chapel Hill—after he got his doctorate. I said, 'Wilson, what are you goin' to school any more for?' He said, 'Mother, you know they's new things and new problems to face,' and said, 'if you don't kindly keep a goin' and sorta keep up,' he said, 'you jest can't do the job.' That's why he went. I didn't think he needed to go after he'd went so much as he had and all, but that's what he said. He said, 'Things change so much that I think you jest have to keep on keepin' on.' "

Mrs. Delia Creech, well along in her seventies and widowed, lives alone in the house she and her husband built at Pine Mountain, Kentucky, sixty years ago. Mrs. Creech raised eight children, one of whom she lost in the Pacific in World War II. Of late years she has been prevailed upon by her children to shut the door of her house and go to Pittsburgh to spend the winter with one of her daughters, who is a physician there. But before the snow is gone in Pittsburgh, Mrs. Creech begins packing her things to go back home. There's her garden to plant and she must get a calf to fatten for the freezer.

As we sat on her front porch high above the dusty road that runs in front of her house, Mrs. Creech told us about earlier days. Schools, she said, began in July and ended in December, and children often had to walk a long distance to the schoolhouse. Six grades were taught in the schools.

"Did any of the students go on to higher schools?" we asked.

"Yes, they did," she said. "They worked to pay their expenses. Got through some way, I don't know how. Sometimes they'd have some cattle they'd sell and they'd work. I don't know how they got through. Just hard work."

Beside the barn across the road, tasseled corn stirred in a gentle breeze.

"What's growing in your garden?" we asked.

"Well, I've got sweet corn," she said, "and field corn, beans, the crease-back and the fall beans, and half-runners, and another kind, and squash, and pumpkin, and okra, pepper, cabbage, and Brussels sprouts, tomatoes, beets, carrots, parsnips. I planted all that. And, oh yes, there's some strawberries and raspberries, and I've got some broccoli, sweet potatoes, Irish potatoes, and rhubarb. I've got onions too."

Mrs. Creech told us how to cook the long strands of dried beans strung on a thread and seen hanging against the wall on the front porch of almost every house in the mountains.

"I cook shucky beans the way my mother did it," she said. "I soak them overnight in cold water. And then I wash them from that water into another water, and put them on to boil awhile,

and after I boil them a little while I change them from that water into another clear, clean water, and put meat with them and salt. A hambone's mighty good with them, but there are just two hambones to a hog, so I usually use fatback. They don't take much of that fat meat to make 'em taste pretty good."

Mrs. Creech and I compared politics on her side of Pine Mountain with the variety I knew as a child on my side of Pine Mountain. There weren't many Democrats on her side of the mountain either, she said. I asked her about election day.

"Oh," she said, "then's when men really cut a shine. They'd have a little booze and then they'd try their guns. Sometimes they'd have a racket and sometimes they wouldn't. Sometimes they'd shoot just to be shootin' and sometimes they kinda took aim. Mostly they shot just to make a noise, but sometimes they shot to kinda kill."

We asked Mrs. Creech if she had attended church as a girl.

"Yes," she said. "We had the Baptist, and another kind of Baptist, and another kind of Baptist. They was one Baptist preacher—I know he was the prejudicest man I ever seen."

Hard work is a commodity that many young people of the mountains today are exchanging for an education, we found at Berea College, Berea, Kentucky, where a well-organized labor program allows students to earn most of their educational expenses. We talked with four outstanding students of the college: Dean Meadows of Kentucky, Ella Crawford of Tennessee, Ceveline Jackson of Alabama, and Carolyn Keith of Virginia.

"My father was a miner," Dean told us. "He had been to a federal school for six weeks and was a registered foreman; so we were a little better off than other miners' families. When I was in the sixth grade the mines began closing down. But because mines employing more than six people have to have a registered foreman, my father was able to find work easily. The mining situation went from bad to worse, however, and when I came to my senior year in high school we were barely getting by.

"I knew in my sophomore year in high school that I wanted to go into the ministry. I knew I would need an education for this, but I had no idea

how to go about getting one. I had never heard of Berea College until a friend of mine applied for admission. I read her catalog and learned about the work program here, and it looked inviting, so I applied too and was accepted. I had seventy-five dollars of my own when I started to Berea. My father borrowed one hundred dollars from a friend. It took twenty-five dollars to get me here. I paid seventy-five dollars on my first term. And that's the only money my parents have given me to pay all my school bills. I've been able to work to pay the others."

Ella, one of ten children and a senior at Berea, had to work against indifference in her family even to get a high school education. But she was encouraged by both her elementary and her high school principals and by the pastor of her church to go to college. By working at whatever odd jobs she could find, she accumulated enough money to enter Berea. Money sent by her pastor helped her stay for several semesters. Then she dropped out of college for a semester and worked in a hosiery mill to earn enough money to allow her to continue her education. When we talked with her, she was looking forward to graduation and to returning to the mountains to teach.

"Do you find that many mountain children are indifferent to education?" we asked.

"Yes," she answered, "but I have ideas for sparking their imaginations."

When Ceveline, daughter of a sharecropper and one of thirteen children, finished high school, she found a job as a daytime waitress and baby-sat at night. A junior high school principal encouraged her to get a good education, and a woman with whose children she baby-sat helped her file an application to Berea.

Ceveline went on a special work program her first semester at Berea, putting in more than the usual number of work hours and taking fewer than the usual number of subjects. With money borrowed from the college, received from two grants, and earned in the summer as a waitress, Ceveline is getting through college.

Asked what she intended to do after graduation, she mentioned a long list of possible careers. She may go back home and teach in order to help other young people go to college. She may apply for admission to the Peace

Corps. Because she is a Negro, she has a desire to work in some African country. And, because she'd like to write sometime, she plans to take courses in creative writing. As for reading, she reads "all the time." She is tremendously interested in psychology. Why? "There are so many things I want to find out about life and about people. Why they hate. Why they dislike."

Carolyn grew up on a Virginia farm, loving every animal on it, and hating butchering season, "when my friends had to be removed from life." The divorce of her parents had been an upsetting experience of her childhood, but she became reconciled to the situation after each parent had married a second time. "Now when I go home I say I'm going to see my four parents," she told us laughingly.

"In the ninth grade, I came to realize I was getting nowhere fast. I wanted to learn and to see and to experience a great many things that I couldn't with the condition my grades were in. So I astounded all my teachers by making the honor roll."

It was then that her high school teachers began to respect her and to hand her responsibility. For two years she worked in the school library and for one year managed the school store. Two of her teachers and her principal encouraged her to apply for admission to Berea where, by working part time, she is majoring in business education.

What will she do with her college education?

"I hope to go back to the mountains to teach. I think the people back home need teachers from their own area who have come up the hard way. By teaching business courses, I can give them something basic, something they can do with their skills when they get out of high school."

At Cumberland is Southeast Community College, one of several junior colleges the University of Kentucky has established over the state. Its enrollment when we visited it was 382 students, most of whom lived within the area and commuted. We talked with Dean Cadle, librarian of the college, Mrs. Jo Cadle of the administration office, and Tom Gaston, formerly of Southeast and now at the Fort Knox Community College.

As an outlander, Gaston gave us his impression of the mountain student and his community.

"I taught here the first three years the college was in operation, from the fall of 1960 through the spring of 1963," he said. "My first impression of the community was that it is characterized by conservatism. It is conservative in terms of family organization; it is conservative in terms of religious orientation; and, in a certain sense, it is conservative politically.

"We find here an authoritarian society in which people tend to want somebody to tell them what to do, and in each of the three fields I mentioned there seems to be someone—a father in the home, a minister in the pulpit, a local politician in the courthouse—who makes the decisions and tells them what to do. The status of the man, not the worth of his ideas, often seems to be most important in determining whether his thinking will be heeded.

"Now of course all this is a purely personal impression, but, if the impression is well grounded, then it is of crucial importance. As a student of language, I think of impressive sociological theory and compelling experimental data which strongly suggest that *the* chief factor in cultural deprivation is the linguistic deprivation that comes with extreme status orientation and authoritarian family control. Children in such situations do not hear their elders defining problems, asking questions, and weighing alternatives. Never hearing the language of problem-solving, they never learn its techniques.

"As a result, it seems to me, students come here as adults having used language almost exclusively for trivial social chitchat, often as a way of avoiding reality, actually, instead of examining it and turning it over in their own minds. We had good students here who left college rather than consider the fact that one might read poetry about such intimate subjects as a man's relation to his wife, regardless of the aim of the poem or its purpose, simply because their religious orientation was such that poetry of this sort couldn't be tolerated. We had one very sincere and hard-working young lady who found the tension aroused by reading Darwin's theory of evolution almost unbearable because so many of her certainties were questioned at the same time.

"All their lives, people in these mountains have been turning away

from reality, and it's a painful thing to undergo a reevaluation of several of one's interlocking certainties at the same time. For the future, the most constructive thing we could do would be to find some way of breaking this cycle of hereditary certainty early, so that students could grow up and enlarge their horizons. It seems to me that Appalachia is apart from what we like to consider as American culture. It is rather self-consciously Appalachia."

Some characteristics of Appalachia Gaston likes.

"I like the fact that not everybody is running all the time and in a hurry. It is by and large a leisurely culture, and that I like. Paradoxically, despite the status orientation, there is more courtesy and consideration, more respect for the autonomy of the individual, here than anywhere else I know."

Gaston cited the inability to read well as the cause for poor classroom performance of many mountain students.

"Many of them I knew to be intellectually capable as far as reasoning is concerned were pushed to the edge of desperation to read through their assignments," he said. "They had little time to read for pleasure."

Because Southeast Community College is a state institution, it is less selective of students than Berea College.

Mrs. Cadle reported that at the end of the spring semester about 23 percent of the freshman students were dropped because of poor grades. An additional 20 percent did not return for the sophomore year. On the other hand, about 85 percent of those who completed the sophomore year went on to other institutions to get college degrees. At the most recent commencement of the University of Kentucky at Lexington, one of Southeast's former students had made Phi Beta Kappa and six had been graduated with honors.

Dean Cadle regretted that few students at the college find time or have the desire to read for pleasure.

"But I do believe this college is making changes in the people here in the mountains," he said. "High school teachers have learned that certain things are going to be expected of their students who enter college here, and I'm sure the quality of instruction in the high schools has improved. We're proud of the records some of our students make at the University."

Perley Ayer, Executive Director of the Council of the Southern Mountains, pointed out to us at his office in Berea that the situation in Southern Appalachia is not unrelated to the values of American culture elsewhere. He does not believe that because this is so we should therefore accept these standards and their consequences. He believes, rather, that we must understand them before we have any hope of successfully improving them.

He told us that through local politics some county school superintendents in the mountains are able to keep themselves and their relatives in office for thirty years or more. Their terms of office may depend more on their skill as politicians than on their ability as school administrators.

"But while we're being a little bit resentful of these people who perpetuate their thrones, we ought to take a look at the values of American culture everywhere at the moment. And what are they? Status and might. So people in political office in the mountains do what about 99 percent of the rest of us are doing elsewhere in one way or another."

Ayer told us of meeting with a group of church members who were considering the responsibility of the church in the war on poverty.

"What they were really asking themselves," Ayer said, "was 'What are we going to do now that these people on relief can outvote us at the polls?' This was the real question that was bothering them.

"One man in the group stood up and said, 'Let's face it. We send our sons and daughters away to college not to learn how to serve the world. We send them away to get the kind of education and the kind of degree and the kind of status that will earn them the most money.'

"In a sort of naïve way I said, 'Well, now, if your purpose is not work because it needs to be done, and well done because it's needed, but is work for whatever society will pay money for, then it would look to me as if this vast number of indigent people who are getting paid for doing nothing are smarter than the rest of you. If you are

saying that work—this good old Protestant work ethic—is good and virtuous because work needs to be done, coal needs to be dug because people need coal, and other things need to be done because they serve a social purpose, this is one thing. But, as you have just said, this is not why you send your kids to college. You send them there to get the most money they can get. It looks to me as if these people who are on relief and are paid to do nothing have a motive which is very similar.' "

Although Ayer recognizes the damage done by strip mining, he "cannot be as angry" with the persons who bought the mineral rights many years ago "as most people are, because they didn't know what they were doing. They were buying the most that they could for the least that they could pay, which is the system we have worked under in America since before I was born. I'm a Yankee by birth, and one of the greatest virtues in New England is held to be getting all that something is worth, or a little more.

"When these long-form deeds were written, nobody ever heard of mining except by digging a hole. And what's a small hole in a field? Now, with the new methods of mining, operators can remove one foot of soil to claim one inch of coal. That's the proportion. So twelve feet of soil to get one foot of coal. So the operators bulldoze about, cover up forests, fill up the streams, and pollute the water.

"Obviously, the men who sold the mineral rights to their property didn't intentionally sell the right to ruin their land in order to dig out the coal. This was beyond their ability to conceive.

"We have the most ridiculous attitude about reclamation of strip-mined areas. It takes nature about 500 years to make an inch of good topsoil. And so we talk about planting a few elderberries up on the strip-mined land and reclaiming it in four or five years."

To the suggestion sometimes made that out-migration is the solution to the problems of Appalachia, Ayer replies, "Out-migration to what? You don't solve a problem just by moving it somewhere else out of sight."

Ayer believes that all men—the affluent, the dominant, the secure, as well as the poor, the dependent, and those without hope—must be led to understand the situation, to recognize their common stake in the future, and

to work together to bring about conditions fair and beneficial to all.

Friends at Redbird Mission had told us that State Senator Durham W. Howard had worked very hard in the Kentucky General Assembly to pass laws placing curbs on strip mining. Senator Howard's name was in my notebook for an interview. We called on him at his office in Pineville.

"The strange thing about strip mining," said the Senator, "is that the courts have held that it is legal under the old long-form contracts, although when the deeds were signed strip mining had not been thought of. I don't agree with that ruling, and I believe that, if opposition to it had been pursued more diligently by property owners and people who had the wherewithal to do it, the court decisions on it would have been different. Certainly, with the conditions that strip mining creates, I don't think that the courts, if they studied the situation diligently, would hold that operators have a right to go in and devastate people's property and to create a hazardous situation for floods. I've got a feeling that eventually the courts will reverse their rulings." To reclaim strip-mined land to any degree of satisfaction would be "utterly impossible," Senator Howard thinks.

We asked him his opinion of a proposal that elderberries should be planted on strip-mined land as a means of reclaiming it.

"Well," he said, "I know something about elderberries. In the first place, they're not a hardy enough plant. I don't think their roots are deep enough to hold the soil. Moreover, I don't think they will grow in this acid soil. That's one of the big problems we're having now—getting anything to grow in this soil. But elderberries, pine trees, and other plants are not going to eradicate the tremendous hazard of flash floods in these strip-mined, cut-over areas.

"I had an office up the street in the '46 flood—I've gone through three floods —and, when the water got six feet deep in my office, I waded over to the Continental Hotel, where I could find a place to rest. The next day a member of the corps of TVA engineers and I were sitting on the hotel porch looking at that water flowing through the town, almost up in the courthouse, and he said to me, 'When you look at the maps of this area and see the tremendous watershed you've got, and your narrow

valleys, you realize that the river could get over the top of that courthouse.' Now I want to live here the rest of my life. I like it here. But you can't live in peace and comfort where that threat is hanging over you."

The Senator expressed the opinion that strip-mined coal could bear a sizable severance tax.

"A severance tax isn't going to wreck the industry," he said. "It isn't going to hurt the coal operators in any way. They come in here and exploit our natural resources today and are gone tomorrow. And they make no contribution to the local community. The TVA is buying this coal entirely too cheaply. It's using a big percentage of stripped coal from this area."

Middlesboro, where coal was being stripped almost within the limits of the city, presented a typical example of a political situation involving strip mining, Senator Howard told us.

"Some of the people of Middlesboro made complaints about it to me as their senator and wanted me to do something about it," he said. "So I looked at the law and found that not only the strip-mining law would give them relief to a certain extent, but that the zoning and planning laws would give them complete relief. When I answered their inquiry, I said, 'You've got the law on the books. You can stop them tomorrow. All you need to do is to tell your officials about it.' The zoning and planning law reaches out five miles beyond the city limits. The city officials of Middlesboro could control any operation that goes on there. They could stop the operators dead cold on that law. But they wouldn't do it because of the politics in it. That's the whole story. It's a political situation. I'll guarantee you they'll never strip any coal within the close proximity of Pineville."

Senator Howard is of the opinion that federal, not state, legislation is the answer to the problem of strip mining and flood control. "It takes the problem a little bit further from the political scene, and people are not as prone to influence other people under federal laws as they are under state laws," he said. "Politics is pretty far reaching in Kentucky," he added.

We asked the Senator if he knew of any popular protest against strip mining.

"Yes," he said. "You may know that a group of people from Pike and some other counties went down to Frankfort and talked to the Governor about the menace of strip mining in their communities. That might be the beginning of a crusade to stop this whole thing. I think if a few more groups of people would organize as these people have up in eastern Kentucky, and let the Governor and the General Assembly know that they're up in arms against strip mining, they'd get some action. Strip mining is unsightly in an area which we are trying to tell people all around is the most beautiful place in the world for visiting and sightseeing and vacationing. And what do visitors see? These unsightly strip-mining scars around the mountaintops. It must be very disappointing to visitors."

Concerning the effectiveness of the Appalachian Regional Development Act, Senator Howard had doubts. "It seems to me this thing is being exploited by politicians," he said, "and the people will derive very little benefit from it in the end. I can see where perhaps the highway program will be very beneficial to us. Outside of that I'd say it's not going to amount to a great deal. I see very little industry coming in here to employ the unemployed. A few towns have, after a long struggle and all kinds of concessions and all kinds of effort, induced a few small factories to come in. But certainly nothing of major consequence."

Only through a process of education that will create a desire within the mountain people to be self-sustaining can they get away from relief programs and government handouts, the Senator believes.

"We're going in the wrong direction," he said. "We have too many people on relief, drawing subsidies of one kind or another. They think they owe allegiance to some politician for their subsidies, and that should never be. They should first be taught that they don't owe me or any other politician anything at all. That's out the window."

Long before we met Dan Gibson, we had heard about him, for he was on the way to becoming a Kentucky mountain legend. Eighty years old, he had successfully defied a sheriff's force to keep bulldozers from a piece of mountain land belonging to one of his stepsons, then with the United States Air Force in Vietnam.

A Baptist preacher for forty-one years,

Dan now makes coffins from trees cut on his mountain acres. We found him finishing a coffin in his little shop beside a twisting road near Fisty, Knott County, where dwindled creeks stink with pollution from mines and spoilbanks. Dan led us past half a dozen coffins in his shop, up a steep slope to his house, where we met his wife, mother of Leonard Ritchie, the stepson who owned the piece of mountain.

Dan had defied the sheriff's force because he considered it a sorry situation that land belonging to a boy fighting in Vietnam should be torn to pieces in his absence, even though the grandfather of the boy had sold the mineral right under a broad-form deed to a coal company.

"Well, first," said Dan, when we asked him about the bulldozer incident, "I'm goin' to tell you the whole story. Hit'll take me a long time." And it did.

Dan watched as the bulldozers moved from Lawson Cornett's place, to Enos Ritchie's, to Charlie Cornett's, to Tigg Ritchie's, to Charmer Barker's (and Barker "a layin' up in Indiana with a stroke of paralysis") until they were close to the line marking the land that belonged to his stepson fighting in Vietnam.

Then, Dan told us, "My stepson-in-law said, 'I'll make you a sign, a no-trespass sign to stick up.' He made the sign, and I started to go up thar where the bulldozers was. Well, I didn't know what they might do and so I took a little old twenty-two gun. You know what a little old twenty-two gun is? I had this sign and it was 30 inches long and 9 inches wide. And a 35-inch piece nailed on it to drive it in the ground. Well, I carried that sign in this hand and the twenty-two in this one. 'Bout ten o'clock I heard 'em when I got in about 150 yards of 'em. And when I got where I could see, there was the deputy sheriff standing 'bout '75 yards in front of these bulldozers. 'Well,' I said, 'I guess I'm up against it.' And so I knew what to do. They didn't care if they hurt me. I walked around the deputy sheriff and come in on him.

"I said, 'What are you a doin' up here?' He said, 'I'm up here a guardin' these men to work.' And I said, 'Mister, I don't want any trouble with you all. I ask you to walk in front of me and go out there and tell them fellers to get off, go back across that line.' Well, he did. And they went back.

"I went out to where my line was, and I couldn't drive the sign up with this crippled hand. I asked a feller a workin' on the bulldozer—he's a mighty nice man—I asked him to drive up the sign. He did. When he got it drove up, I said, 'Now, gentlemen, I don't want any trouble with you.' I said, 'As long as you stay over on that side there'll be no trouble. But,' I said, 'don't cross this no more.' Well, they went about a hundred yards and all of 'em set down.

"Well, this boss, he has a radio on his truck, and so he radioed into headquarters. That was about ten o'clock. I set thar until about two o'clock, and nobody showed up. Then my step grandson and a neighbor boy came to me and said, 'Grandpa, you haven't had any dinner, have you?' And I said, 'No, I haven't.' 'Well, do you want us to bring you some dinner and some water?' I said, 'All right.' I said, 'Yes, and some cigarettes.' I give 'em two one-dollar bills and they came offen the hill. My wife fixed dinner, sent me a good dinner and water. The boys came back with it. I was eatin' dinner, and they was twenty men settin' between me and these boys.

"Then all at onct I seed six officers come around this point, cross the sign, and come over. They walked up about thirty steps, and one of 'em was Sergeant Mitchell. And he said, 'We've come after you.' And I said, 'What for?' He said, 'We're takin' you out of here.' I said 'I ain't goin' no place.' 'What! You mean to tell me you're not goin?' I said, 'No. You heard what I said.' 'Well, we've come after you.' I said, 'Sergeant Mitchell, didn't you see that sign right back thar? No trespassin'? Didn't you pass it?' He said, 'Yes, I did.' 'Well,' I said, 'what are you a doin' over here on other people's land? Tryin' to run me off my own property?' He said, 'I've got a right to be here.' And I said, 'Well, I'm eighty years old —I'm a goin' on eighty-one years old— and I never in my life had no trouble with nobody—never. But,' I said, 'we have got tired of you fellers runnin' over our homes to destroy 'em.' And I said, 'I don't care to die, even if you do.' I said, 'Do you want to die?' 'No, I don't,' he said. 'Well,' I said, 'all right, you just move back beyond that sign and they won't be no trouble.' Well, they went back."

A few hours later, three of Dan's friends, two of them members of the Appalachian Committee to Save the Land and the People, talked Dan off the mountain. They had heard that forty men from the sheriff's force and the state patrol were on the way up with a warrant for Dan's arrest and they feared violence.

"Well, these boys came up and I was still a settin' there," Dan told us. "One of 'em hollered to me. He says, 'Dan, I want to talk to you.' I said, 'O.K.' And I walked down to where they were. The old Combs man from Lotts Creek, he said, 'Come walk down the hill with me.' He said, 'No tellin' how long they'll be here, and I'm afraid they'll kill ye. Or you'll kill some of them.' 'Well,' I said, 'If they shoot me, I'll shore get some of 'em if I can. I ain't goin' to do it 'thout they do it.' And I said, 'I'm not a leavin' here. This is our land. Hit's turrible for a person to be run off his own property.' Well, they begged and begged, and finally I turned around and give 'em my gun and I said, 'Well, I'll go with ye.' "

But Dan did not leave the mountain until one of his friends, Eldon Davidson, Principal of the high school at Jenkins and Secretary of the Appalachian Committee to Save the Land and the People, had talked to the officers and extracted from them a promise to respect the no trespassing sign.

Dan was taken out of his own district to Sassafras before a magistrate who was an employee of a coal company. But Dan "knew a few things about courts." He told the magistrate, "I know you're out of your jurisdiction." He was placed in jail for about an hour. But when the town began filling up with people who had heard about the arrest, Dan was released. He was later taken before a county judge at Hindman, where a restraining order was placed on him and on the coal operator to stay off the stepson's land for one month.

We asked Dan if he thought the Appalachian Committee to Save the Land and the People was an effective organization.

"We've had a good lot of effect so far," he said. "We shore have. We've got a promise from the Governor. We've got a promise from President Johnson. We've got a promise from Carl Perkins, our state senator, and we have promises from representatives. I called Governor Breathitt myself before this motorcade of sixty-nine cars went to Frankfort.

"I went right with 'em to Frankfort and set right in the Governor's office and talked with him, as close to me as that gentleman." He nodded his head toward Edward.

Dan pointed to a neighboring mountain where, he told us, the overburden from a strip mine had washed down into the front yard of a friend of his.

"And comes a rain," Dan said, "that overburden's goin' to slide down into the bottom. This country out here, if it is stripped any more, ever'body that's a livin' here is a goin' to have to leave here. That's a settled-down proposition. We'll have to leave."

"Where will you go?" I asked.

"Well, shore enough," he said, "where will we go?"

Dr. and Mrs. Lundy Adams of Blackey, Kentucky, active in the Appalachian Committee to Save the Land and the People, drove us in their jeep up on a mountain to see where strip mining and augering had been in progress. After we had surveyed the devastation before us—thousands of trees, many of them large, and millions of tons of soil pushed down the mountainside—we looked toward the west at another mountain, the top of which belonged to Dr. and Mrs. Adams. Dr. Adams told us it had once been the farm of his grandfather and that as a boy he had spent many happy hours there. The farm had passed out of the family, but for sentimental reasons the Adams had bought it a few years ago and had planned to spend their retirement years there—until they had been given notice that the owner of the mineral rights would soon move in to begin strip mine operations.

"People need to understand the far-reaching effects of strip mining right now," said Dr. Adams. "It must be controlled through legislation now and not ten years from now, not five years from now, not one year from now, but right now."

"We love the mountains," Mrs. Adams told us. "We're here by choice. We chose our house seat at the very summit of the mountain where we could look out into the distance and see all the colors in autumn and the snow in winter, the dogwoods and redbuds in spring. Then my husband started to replant the orchards that he had remembered on his grandfather's farm. He started with a peach orchard. He took the rails that his own father had cut over fifty years ago and built a

rail fence around our cabin. Below our cabin was the stump where his mother sat when his father asked her to marry him fifty-eight years ago.

"So you see the love of the land is there. It is deep. I feel that my husband stayed here to serve his people because he loved them. We wanted to spend our remaining years on this piece of land. And now all that will be changed by giant equipment that will go in there and tear and destroy."

Dr. Adams spoke of the ruined water supply as one of the far-reaching effects of strip mining. Land denuded by strip mining permits quick runoff of surface water, resulting in a lowered water table and a deficient water supply. Acid-contaminated water from strip mines mingles with water in underground streams and contaminates wells drilled for drinking water.

"Recently, seven wells have been dug in the vicinity of my office, six of which have been bad," Dr. Adams related. "Thousands of dollars have been spent in drilling wells and trying to find potable water. At last, I'm told, we have a well that is producing good water, but I notice my new lavatory, which was put in only two weeks ago, is already highly stained with iron sulfide."

Dr. Adams pointed out to us the reclamation which, according to Kentucky law, every strip-mine operator under bond must make when he leaves a stripped area. It consisted of a few spindly blades of grass growing in one spot on a huge pile of overburden at the edge of a road along the bench.

The economic ills of the mountains have had a permanently harmful effect upon the people, Dr. Adams believes.

"I was born and reared in this section of the mountains," he told us. "I remember our people from my boyhood that they were very independent, self-reliant, individualistic. They would not accept anything from a neighbor unless they returned it and more. If they borrowed a cup of sugar, they returned two cups. All this changed about the years 1930 to 1932. These people—it seems that even their character and personalities changed. In the '27 flood, which was our worst, I remember no one in the area would accept help from the Red Cross. They would be asked questions,

'How much fencing did you have destroyed?' 'What did the flood do to your outbuildings?' 'How much bottom land did you lose?' The answer was always polite but curt. 'I lost a little fence here and a little bottom land there, but I'll take care of that. I want no help from you.'

"Then we had a flood in '37, and some people accepted help. Of course you remember in the thirties we had PWA and WPA, which people took advantage of. They had to because of the depression. Along about that time there set in what some of us old-timers believe to be a deterioration of character.

"Down through the years, more and more and more people took advantage of all of the programs that were set up to take care of the really very poor. Now we have a new syndrome that we in the medical profession have termed a chronic passive dependency syndrome. I hear it's found outside the mountains, too. I do not know about that. Many mountain people now are prone to depend on give-away programs, foodstuffs that are handed out, the food stamp program. They have imaginary ills. Fully 75 to 90 percent have psychosomatic illness, which is nothing more than an illness without a disease. A good portion of the able-bodied people will not work. I'm speaking now of the men. In this region the woman is the backbone of the family. The husband complains of real or imaginary illness and he sits on the porch and whittles or tells tall tales and chews his tobacco. The wife goes out and makes a living.

"The gifted, the young, the energetic, the ambitious have gone from the region," continued Dr. Adams. "Our literacy rate right at the present time, I believe, is about 6.3 grade-wise. The children have caught on to the gimmick of the government owing us a living, and they drop out of school, or attempt to, at an early age. Their ambition seems to be to get on some welfare program. They are encouraged in this by their parents. The children are anxiety ridden. Frequently we pick up duodenal ulcers in the children. They have neurotic diseases, and they don't get along well in school. All of this happening to my people here in the mountains I highly resent, because I believe and am firmly convinced that our federal government must carry the blame for what has been done to the people here.

"Some of the children are pitiful beings. Your heart goes out to them when you see them in the office. A lot of them have intestinal parasites. They have carious teeth. They are plagued with the difficulties of getting along in their homes. They hear nothing but complaints from their parents. The symptomology of their parents is reiterated perhaps hundreds of times daily, until it is seared into the consciousness of the children. If a mother is anxiety ridden, her children will be. Many times we discover actual pathology."

We asked Dr. Adams if he thought the introduction of industries into the mountains would cure the economic and social ills.

"Any industries brought into the mountains would have to be small," he said. "We don't have the space and we don't have the water for large industries. The solution to the water situation will be surface water— reservoirs. We people are not able to build reservoirs. State and federal governments should build reservoirs for storage of water in the mountains. These reservoirs could supply water for towns. They could supply water for the small industries for which we could find space.

"If the federal government would come in and move all of the people from the heads of the hollows to central locations and keep them there, if it would take over the areas between these centers of population, perhaps twenty or thirty miles apart, and make the region into a national forest, permit no cutting of timber, reforest the area and restock it with game, and bring in engineers to throw up dams and give us plenty of reservoir water, and turn the region into a recreation spot, I believe it could be restored. Let the tourists come in. We'd have to turn some of these mountaintops into heliports. We could teach the mountain people working in motels and restaurants how to meet the public, how to make beds, how to hang a clean towel on the rack in the room where a tourist is going to stay, how to bait the tourist's hook, and then bait the tourist. That way they could make a living, and people from Ohio and Illinois and New York or wherever they live could come in here for their recreation and their fishing, and go back to their businesses refreshed."

James Still, poet, novelist, and author

of numerous short stories about mountain people, makes his home between the waters of Dead Mare Branch and Wolfpen Creek in Knott County. For many years he was librarian at the Hindman Settlement School at the forks of Troublesome Creek, during which time he initiated the bookmobile program in the county. He recalls with gratitude that he was able to put at least a quarter of a million good books into the hands of children. He now teaches at Morehead State University, Morehead, Kentucky.

"Our land has been ruined, the streams polluted," said Mr. Still as we visited in his apartment on the Morehead campus. "After it's all gone, and not worth saving, after it's a wasteland, we'll have laws and rules and regulations—too late. And this business of planting pokeberries, or fescue, or apple trees, or ground covers is a farce. I feel ashamed when I hear such ideas proposed as a solution. Are we considered so simple-minded? The solution is to stop now. Now! While we have something. It won't matter in three or four years the way it's going. It hardly matters now where I live. It hardly matters. The creek in front of my house is filled with mud. Nowadays we have no clear streams, no fish. Mud and slime and mine acid. The blasting behind my house when a road was built disturbed the underground water channels and my well went dry last summer for the first time in all reckoning. In the fall the water rose, but to a lower level, and with its taste altered. I haul water for drinking from the well of a neighbor.

"It might have been a master idea if somebody had started years ago to turn the mountains into a park land, but I suppose it would have sounded visionary then. With the mountains cut down—who will choose to come down to look at the Cola signs? The Cola signs and all the trash and discarded automobiles and junk piles? There's nothing here to see. I know I'll stay the rest of my life. I'll adjust. I'll cope. But the life I knew is gone. I feel something for these mountains. I feel something here that I can't experience anywhere else."

All over the mountains of Kentucky we found angry people. In Hazard, there was Mrs. Francie Hager, a volunteer worker for the Appalachian Committee for Full Employment. We found Mrs. Hager in what appeared to be an abandoned warehouse, serving then as

the office of the organization, which was headed by Berman Gibson, an unemployed miner and an eloquent spokesman for the unemployed.

"The purpose of the committee," Mrs. Hager told us, "is to bring industries into Perry County and to the other mountain parts of Kentucky for the poor people so that they can have work—so that they can make a living and get off of charity. We appreciate what people do for us, but we don't want to spend the rest of our lives on charity.

"And we want industries such as factories and things like that to come in here so that we can have jobs to work at and can live like other people, and not be ashamed of ourselves when the out-of-state people come in and see us."

She complained that influential persons in the community, many of them coal operators, were not interested in bringing in industry.

"They want motels and hotels," she said, "and swimmin' pools and recreation halls for the youth, and things like that that won't be of any specific help to the poor class of people." She told us of a huge motel on top of a nearby mountain.

"I say, if they can climb to the top of a mountain and knock the top of that mountain off and put a million-dollar motel up there, then they can knock the top of a mountain off and put us a million-dollar factory up there that would employ a lot of unemployed people.

"Our water supply—at times it does pretty good. But since they've done so much of this strippin' and augerin' . . . You see all this debris that they tore up on those mountains. When it comes a hard rain, it washes it off and washes it down into our streams and hit pollutes 'em so bad we don't have fish. Even fish don't live in these streams here. They have a new water plant here, but hit's not a doin' a good job on puttin' out good water."

Mrs. Hager told us that a single person on relief in her area was receiving twelve dollars a month in food stamps. These stamps, which represented the individual's entire income from relief, were issued on payment of two dollars in cash. Some people were having great difficulty in accumulating the two dollars, she said.

In Whitesburg, Kentucky, near which my father grew up reading the *Mountain Eagle,* we talked with the present editor of this weekly—young, mountain-born, courageous, crusading Tom Gish.

Gish is outspokenly critical of what he considers the disproportionately large amount allocated for roads under the Appalachian Regional Development Act.

"As a good program for eastern Kentucky I increasingly go back to the old business of education," Mr. Gish told us. "I think that the root of most of our troubles is the lack of a good educational system. This lack can be traced to absentee ownership of our resources. When the sons and daughters of the people who own the wealth are not here, then the people who own the wealth are not interested in good schools in our area. Owners of the wealth have succeeded in keeping taxes down so that our local taxes are virtually nonexistent, and state taxes and even federal taxes on eastern Kentucky resources are so very, very small as to be nonexistent for all practical purposes. The writer of an article in a recent issue of a business magazine says that the leasing of coal land in eastern Kentucky is the most profitable business in the United States.

"TVA is the biggest user of strip-mined coal. To me, it's absolutely nonsense for the federal government to create and support an agency such as the TVA in the name of helping the people of a given section of the country and then use that very same agency to rape and rob and pillage in another section, which is what they're doing. TVA, whether it admits it or not, is subsidizing wholesale robbery.

"I very much favor a severance tax, and I believe the proposal would have wide support, even within the coal industry, among larger, more informed, more intelligent operators. Of course, it would get some standardized points of opposition, as you would expect, but I have had three or four of the major operators tell me privately that they know we should have had a severance tax fifty years ago, and still we do not have one."

Larry Craft, on the faculty of Southeast Community College, Cumberland, and Judith, his wife, both mountain-born, agree with Tom Gish that education is an important ingredient in the cure